Cameroon's industrial policies since 1945

Hope, disillusion and utopia

Samuel BIROKI

Cameroon's industrial policies since 1945

Hope, disillusion and utopia

L'Harmattan
Cameroun

Du même auteur

Les politiques industrielles du Cameroun depuis 1945. Espoir, désillusion et utopie, L'Harmattan, 2021.

5-7, rue de l'Ecole-Polytechnique, 75005 Paris

http://www.editions-harmattan.fr

ISBN : 978-2-343-23812-8
EAN : 9782343238128

AKNOWLEDGEMENTS

To my beloved late mother Martha, father Paul, and my younger sister Sarah, for their sacrifices that built up my character and my generosity towards mankind, and equally for their wishes in my professional and social growth. As your dreams and prayers are getting to accomplishment, may your memories last for ever!

To my lovely wife, Evelyne BIROKI, whose patience has been once again tested during the writing of this Essay, for nights and weekends of unavailability! Your unconditional support, understanding and appropriate meals gave me strength and stand precious for the success of our large family. You are the love of my life.

I also wish to thank all those who are sharing my destiny and the constant change in my prospects as a man of faith that God has blessed abundantly.

OUTLINE

FOREWORD

For years, thinkers, actors and observers of the economy of Cameroon have been concerned about the depleting production of industrial analysis essays. To fill this void, academics, researchers, teachers, senior executives of economic administrations or companies, politicians or political party headquarters are very often content with assumptions, statements and comments.

This book will undoubtedly be received with real curiosity, scientifically and politically speaking. Reading it will certainly bring relief and certainty, as issues raised are treated, despite the seriousness with an independent mind-set.

It seemed useful to me to probe history by organizing an exploration over a period of seventy-five (75) years (1945-2020), through theories, strategies, experiments, and expectations. It was necessary to combine analytical approach, courage of criticism with global knowledge. Readers of different sensitivities will have enough to document their doubts or convictions. In any case, they will be able to appreciate the daring masterpiece within a formidable wilderness, thanks to features derived from academic background and professional experience.

This brainchild is singularly distinguished by its pedagogical aspect. Tools for Cameroon's industry, kind of "**archaeological dig**", helped unveil the experiences of successive governments without hesitation, very often by trial and error. The failures recorded do not owe anything to chance. Appropriate markers will help to illuminate the obstacles that have marked the path of the country's industrialization. Besides the governmental utopia embodied in the **Vision 2035**, there is another one, based on **praxis** and **realism**, in an attempt to provide answers to the thorny questions raised by the under-industrialization of Cameroon, a country rich in human, mining, land, ecological and financial resources.

Therefore, the underlying question at stake is to know why industrialization policies that have been successful elsewhere failed in Cameroon.

One tentative answer: because of an inefficient and corrupt bureaucracy!

From this point on, there is serious doubt about the chances of success of current or anticipated initiatives, as there is no indication of a fundamental change in economic and institutional governance. However, the problem of Cameroon's industrialization should therefore be tackled "**with a chainsaw, not with a nail file**". Hence the little risk I take of dissociating myself from preconceived ideas and the Milky Way that leads to emergence.

Contradictory and constructive debate on Cameroon's industrial policies is therefore being rekindled. The hope is that it will incubate a successful industrialization model that can be duplicated by countries that have similar paths or deemed comparable in their economic and social processes.

This objective will certainly be achieved, as long as no one tries to be right against all odds. If this work succeeds in becoming part of the chronicles of the applied economy, it will undoubtedly be able to help politicians, sector actors, lecturers, analysts, researchers, specialists/consultants, students in economic sciences, management, political sciences, law, finance, engineering professions, architects, town planners, industrialists, finance operators, bankers as well as the civil society to form a precise opinion on the industrialization process of a country.

Dr Samuel BIROKI

AFRICAN PUBLIC FINANCE APPROACH OF CAMEROON'S INDUSTRIAL POLICIES

THEORETICAL AND PRACTICAL REMARKS OF A HETERODOX POLITICAL ECONOMY

The book entitled, *"Industrial Policies in Cameroon since 1945: Hope, Disillusionment and Utopia"* by Doctor Samuel BIROKI, whose drafting was completed in December 2019, is a real source of applied industrial economics.

The author mobilizes his educational and intellectual as well as professional and functional resources to provide a reasoned, documented and located view of the configuration and evolution of Cameroon's industrial policies, both temporal and structural, since 1945 (moments of consciousness of autonomy and political independence), until the projected moment of political empowerment and independence materialized by the successful economic emergence.

Samuel BIROKI presents himself as an honest man, using his experience and his culture of the economy to put industrial policies in Cameroon in a rational perspective.

The author defines himself mainly as an experienced practitioner and established technician rather than a master thinker and theoretician-scientist, with no ambition to propose an academic draft. However, the rationale that governs Samuel BIROKI's work is based on a particular theoretical purpose, which corresponds to Kant's Practical Theory. This means that the author implements a technically regulated aim of normative and pragmatic theorization of the socio-historical trajectory of Cameroon's industrial policies as key economic policies.

In his essay, Samuel BIROKI unfolds the course of Cameroon's industrial history with an expert and practitioner insight. In doing so, he undertakes to revisit, from a critical historical chronicle perspective, the political, industrial and economic-industrial path of Cameroon, based on a practical and technical examination of the path of Cameroon's industrial policies concerning a key area of economic activity.

The sceptical pragmatism that Samuel BIROKI displays and claims encourages him to adopt a historical and eclectic approach which wanders from any dogmatic orientation in reviewing the problem developed.

Samuel BIROKI's pragmatic commitment leads him to adopt a heterodox standpoint which advocates minimizing schemes of dogmatic orientation and issues in his writing on the genesis and dynamics of Cameroon's industrial policies. His work then becomes a simultaneously practical and civic venture to evaluate public policies on the creation, development, strengthening or selection of industrial niches as located and contextualized paths to economic development.

Samuel BIROKI uses an analytical and intellectual toolbox, built in a logic that was primarily concerned with adjusting his vision to the empirical and historical data characteristic of the industrial policy path.

Samuel BIROKI designed, conceived and wrote his essay with the aim of presenting an original and clean analysis, capable of contextualizing and adapting the documented reflection and investigation on the organic, technical, strategic and practical process of industrial policies in Cameroon. In doing so, the author presented a careful study of the structuring and transformation of industrial policies, their conceptual and doctrinal references, as well as their real practical references.

This bias, taken for an informed but also committed look at Cameroon's industrial trajectory, does not prevent the author from sketching a normative and programmatic framework in order to reorient and redeploy the engineering of Cameroon's industrial policies.

Samuel BIROKI does not simply repeat a historical and descriptive examination of Cameroon's industrial development. He is not limited to a critical review of Cameroon's industrial policies. He also takes on the task of reformulating on the basis of reformist optimism, of building a normative, corrective and prospective imagination, using a reconstructive utopia in a didactic way. The aim is to design, formulate and structure the desirable and commendable lines of action and decision participating in an informed and appropriate strategic foresight; which would be able to ensure with intelligence and relevance, the definition of decision-making and action scenarios capable of usefully contributing to the revival, repositioning and redeployment of the economy of Cameroon through the construction of a propelling industrial growth and power.

The author's display refers to a self-presentation in which he intends to demonstrate pragmatic neutralism and agnostic scepticism, all provisions designed to ensure the intellectual autonomy and independence necessary to carry out a critical review of industrial policies in Cameroon in a stripping manner.

However, upon analysis, a demanding reading of this test cannot be satisfied with such a display. In fact, Samuel BIROKI has many inclinations about the paradigmatic choices of industrial policies in Cameroon, as shown by his predilection for a political economy of rationalized **neo-mercantilism**. This is the very reason why he chose the eminent theorist John Maynard Keynes as his inspirational figure. Basically, even if Samuel BIROKI does not manifest it loudly, John Maynard Keynes is an important figure for him; who refers to his own conception of the political economy of industrialization and industrial consolidation in Cameroon.

Samuel BIROKI also underlines his predilection for structured industrial governance, ensured by the call for a popularized and coordinated capitalism.

The author underlines his commitment to an industrial policy based on Patriotic State Regulation, which builds the steering of industrial policies as public policies oriented towards the institutionalization and organization of rational and relational capitalism. For him, it is thus a matter of pleading in favour of a capitalism of competence and consistency, and militating for the downgrading of a capitalism of complacency and connivance.
Samuel BIROKI appears as he is in himself, once the attentive reader tears the veil of his doctrinal neutralism; he is a persistent humanist. In fact, he is a temperate anti-conformist, because he does not use his critical apprehension of industrial policies in Cameroon to allow himself to drift towards **desperate radicalism**. This is why this moderate heterodox uses didactically reconstructive utopia to rebuild a **path of hope and expectations** that makes it possible to envisage the success of a new bet on Cameroon's industrial policies. This work, despite its massive stature, proceeds to a historical-cultural and historical-structural archaeology of industrial policies and strategies in Cameroon. The author succeeds in combining topical examination, critical analysis, canonical formulation, pragmatic sense and utopian constructivism.

That said, we can point out as a weakness of Samuel BIROKI's essay on Industrial Competitiveness in Cameroon, the often uneven division of parts and chapters, and an often rhapsodic construction of the subject. It is also regrettable that, in order to avoid the shortcomings related to the spirit of the system, the author has refrained from building, according to a canonical logic, a political and decisional package, proposing elaborated, informed and tooled measures. Such a system-strategic and strategy-prospective set of measures would have given political-bureaucratic and political-managerial consistency to its regulatory utopianism, by concretely giving a new horizon of intelligence and relevance to Cameroon's industrial policies.

Despite these limitations, there is no doubt that Samuel BIROKI's essay will contribute to the deepening of the technical debate, but also of the citizen debate on the institutional, organizational, conventional, operational, action-oriented and decision-making choices on the basis of which industrial policies in Cameroon are formulated and formalized, then applied, materialized and executed. This essay, even if it is part of a practical theory of industrial policy in Cameroon since 1945, may suggest that, university specialists (economists, political scientists, lawyers, sociologists, psychologists, anthropologists, geographers or historians) are well versed in pure theory or pure practical theory.

Samuel BIROKI's reflection reveals and expresses the emergence of a rationality in the arts of Government, which is shaped by the concern to contextualize and adapt the examination of industrial competitiveness in Cameroon, taking into account a view that is both historian and historicist and attentive to national peculiarities. By operating in this way, he paves the way for a practical theorization of industrial policies in Cameroon, thus contributing to the emergence of practical and technical forms of analytical rationalization of economic policies and political economy in Cameroon. In this way, he highlights the rising and emerging construction of a public policy rationality of power and government inscribed and transcribed in an African context.

Committed and iconoclastic author, Samuel BIROKI is considered a fascinated archaeologist of the complexity of industrial sediments that allowed him to build his utopia on the industrialization of Cameroon as well as the conditions for its materialization. His essay crosses the boundaries of the pragmatic register of instrumental sciences that are the auxiliary sciences of government to be located on rational anticipations of emergence sheltered from any dogmatic speculation.

Professor Mathias Éric OWONA NGUINI

Vice-Rector of University of Yaounde I in charge of Research, Cooperation & Relationship with the World of Entreprises
Paul ANGO ELA Foundation of Geopolitics

ABSTRACT

There are numerous ways to bring Cameroon to the elite of emerging countries by 2035. On the government side, the reference framework is still the same even though subject to revision. Besides the security dimension, the challenge for public authorities is to find enough resources to finance the Growth and Employment Strategy Paper (GESP) adopted in 2009, improve the business environment, protect the national economic space, accelerate decentralization, modernize public administration and promote performance-based management. All these require institutional, structural and organizational reforms.

The downward variation in some macroeconomic aggregates, as well as the reversibility observed in the social field show that there are significant efforts to be made to close the gaps and restore the economy to the growth path set out in the 2035 Vision and the GESP. The private sector complains about tax injustice, a business climate plagued by corruption, long delays in the payment of services to the State, economic gloom, and marked by non-compliance with the Government's commitments under the public-private partnership (PPP). Foreign investors fear the ever-increasing country risk due to the crisis in the English-speaking Regions, attacks by the armed sect BOKO HARAM in the Far-North, and growing insecurity in the Adamawa Region.

The Civil Society is concerned about the deterioration of social indicators, namely in the areas of health, unemployment and underemployment, but more generally in the human development index. This concern is fuelled by the poor prospects for improving the living conditions and incomes of the population, the persistence of poverty and the worsening of categorical, territorial, wage and sector-based inequalities, and uncertain access to employment for young graduates. The Civil Society also deplores the widespread corruption in the social sector and the misappropriation of public funds, which undermine the effectiveness of policies and financing, while depriving the country of investment opportunities in social infrastructure.

Thus, to cope with the economic difficulties that are worsening under the combination of commodity price volatility and political uncertainty, a consensus is emerging on the diversification of agricultural, industrial and mining sectors, as well as on the profitability of value chains.

Cameroon's Industrial Policy at the beginning of the 21st century was based on the logic of intervention built on: Three (03) Harbours: Digital; Agro-industry; Energy; Five (05) Strategic Industrial Pillars: Textile/Confection; Mining and Metallurgy; Forest/Wood; Hydrocarbons and Petro-chemistry; Chemicals and Pharmaceuticals; Two (02) Foundations: Infrastructure and Financing; One (01) Sailing boat: Strategic Watch and Business Intelligence.

The competitiveness of Cameroon's economy depends twice on its strategic positioning on the ECCAS (Economic Community of Central African States) and Nigeria markets, and on a combat architecture focused on three challenges to be met in the Central African Region (CEMAC/ECCAS) and Nigeria, namely, in the medium and long term, to become: (i) the Switch, (ii) the Feeder and (iii) the Equipment Manufacturer in this geographical area.

Thanks to a glance in the past and the appraisal of the policies in progress, this work aims to point out the failures in industrial process during the years before and after the independence, and the potential to miss or reach the announced rendezvous. It also reveals why Cameroon did not become a performing industrial country despite the strategies experienced. Featuring challenges after digging the mine of industrial sediments, it shows how to bridge the gaps and face the stakes to reach or not the Middle-income country step. Starting from the year 1945, the end of World War II, Cameroon's Industrial planners drew their way by trial and error, but a strategic based on imitation.

Before the political freedom was acquired, public authorities, with the support of the French technical assistance, implemented twice, a 4-year development plan (1946-1950 and 1956-1960). Liberalism was the rule of trans-border business in Cameroon, mapped by the **"Open Doors Policy".** After the independence, the 5-year Plan was implemented to structure an inclusive and participative development process. The first Plan started in 1961 and ended in 1966 with a hopeful report. Since then, things started moving differently with the **Planned Liberalism,** an ideology conceived to frame the social and economic emancipation. The **Industrialization by Imports/Substitution Strategy** was endowed with financial and operational means to take off. During the second 5-year Plan (1966-1971), this strategy was coupled with the **Industrialization by Promotion of the Exports**. The 6th 5-years Plan started in 1986, the main economic indicators being to the green. That optimistic situation did not evolve a cause of an economic crisis that exploded in 1987. Since then, international economic doctors came to the bed head of Cameroon to prescribe some therapies without deepened diagnosis.

In 1989, the **Structural Adjustment Plan (SAP)** was written within a context of the public finance stabilization. After Cameroon was declared as a **High Indebted Poor Country (HIPC)** in 1997, a **Poverty Reduction Strategic Paper** (PRSP) was prepared by the Cameroonian government and approved by the international financial community in 2003. However, things did not work as well as expected, the handicaps being: slowness, bureaucracy and corruption in public administration and other institutions. Given a weak competitive framework, measures taken for the social and economic improvement did not bring any significant progress. Consequently, in 2009, the government imagined the Vision to make Cameroon an **Emerging Country by the 2035 horizon.** Three of the four goals adopted frame with the emergence:

i. Becoming a middle-income country ;
ii. Acquiring the status of Newly Industrialized Country ;

With competitiveness as a challenge, Cameroon is called to **do business not as usual**. Out of that, the vision of emergence will remain a dream that will never come true. That is to engage economy in the ways that improve creativity, productivity and innovation, leaning on technological dynamics to boost industrial development. One of the paths of success certainly depends on breaking the structures that maintain the socio-economic duality; more particularly, to change policies and strategies, through audacious reforms, and a leadership and management mastery.

INTRODUCTION

"Competitiveness" is one of the most commonly used concepts in economics but it is not precise enough. The term originated from the Classical Latin word "petere" meaning to seek, attack, **aim** at, desire, and the Latin prefix "con-" meaning together. The German expression for competitiveness, "Wettbewerbsfähigkeit" is, "the *ability* to compete". Historically, the term competitiveness has been used primarily to draw attention to the cost position of firms or countries. Traditionally, analyses of outcome competitiveness examine GDP per capita as well as employment and unemployment rates (Aiginger, 2006). The classical approach focuses mainly on competitiveness at the macro-level (international, country, regional), whereas the neoclassical approach on the micro-level (companies and firms). The phrase was coined in the 70s of the twentieth century. It was then that American economists, under the evidence of severe trade battle between American and Japanese companies, undertook the first attempts to determine the degree of competitiveness between the rival economies [Wziątek-Kubiak 2003].

There is a wide range of definitions of competitiveness to clarify this term. For Barker, Köhler [1998]: Country's competitiveness is the degree to which it can, under free and fair market conditions, produce goods or services meeting the test of international markets, while simultaneously maintaining and expanding the real incomes of its population over the longer term. Ajitabh, Momaya [2004]: Competitiveness of a firm is its share in the competitive market. Bobba et al. [1971] Competitiveness is the ability of nations, regions and companies to generate wealth being the precondition for high wages. Buckley et al. [1988] a firm's competitiveness means its ability to produce and sell products and services of superior quality and lower costs than its domestic and international competitors. Altomonte et al. [2012] External or international competitiveness is the ability to exchange the goods and services that are abundant in home country for the goods and services that are scarce in this country. Flejterski [1984] Competitiveness is the capacity of the sector, industry or branch to design and sell its goods at prices, quality and other features that are more attractive than the parallel characteristics of the goods offered by the competitors. Krugman [1990, 1994] if competitiveness has any meaning, it is simply just another way to express productivity. According to Michael Porter [1990] the only meaningful concept of competitiveness at the national level is national productivity. Scott, Lodge [1985] National competitiveness is a country's ability to create, produce, distribute goods and/or services in international trade while earning rising returns on its resources. Competitiveness is also "a set of institutions, policies, and factors that determine the level of productivity of a country" World Economic Forum WEF [1996].

Cost competitiveness focus on wages as the main cost component, but they also extend to energy prices and taxes, and capabilities generated by innovation (*Aiginger,* 2006). "Quality competitiveness" or "technological competitiveness" is used to describe two specific aspects (quality and technology).

The core debate about the term competitiveness has not changed very much since the early 1990s; it continues to follow the path outlined above. The productivity-based view of competitiveness aims to shed light on the underlying drivers of the standard of living in a particular location. But how should 'standard of living' be measured?

It turns out that this is far more than a technical question; it is an issue with significant impact on policy implications from the analysis. The traditional analysis has used some variation of GDP per capita as the core 'dependent variable' to capture the level of prosperity and productivity allocation has achieved. Purchasing power adjustments are usually made to get a better sense of the goods and services a location can afford given its income Beyond-GDP measures aim to capture non-income related factors that influence the standard of living in a society. There is a range of ranking official institutions like the OECD, the World Economic Forum (the World Competitiveness Index), the World Bank (Doing Business), the UNDP (Social Progress Index) and other groups that have a similar ambition. The ultimate measure of success is an increase in the standard of living." From these definitions, the concept may refer to different levels of aggregation: supranational, national, regional, local, industrial, sectorial, and companies (or farms). Therefore, competitiveness reveals itself as multidimensional and often interchangeably with other concepts like productivity, innovation or market share.

According to Porter and Rivkin [2012], the wide misunderstanding of the concept of competitiveness has dangerous consequences for political discourse as well as policy and corporate choices that are all also evident today.

CHAPTER I:

THE EMERGENCE OF THE CAMEROON ECONOMY AS A NATIONAL CHALLENGE

Cameroon is a country that has a great potential of growth. To become an emerging economy means investing in more productive capacity to get a rapid economic growth due to changes in markets, technology, business culture and social practices. In this prospect, it has to create a better quality of life for its people thanks to the processing its natural materials and adopting industrialization and free market or mixed economy. The position of an upper-intermediate country Cameroon is striving to reach by the 2035 horizon is the one with a GDP per capita more than USD 4036 a year, or 2, 4 million CFA francs. Given that in 2018, the GDP per capita in Cameroon was USD 1,400 (1,330 in 2015). Thus, between 2015 and 2035, the GDP per capita must grow from 784.700 CFA francs to 2, 4 million CFA francs per annum, representing an annually medium increase of 80,750 FCFA. According to the World Bank, to reach that GDP objective, Cameroon economy must grow 8% annually for 20 years; that requires an investment growth rate moving up from 20 to 30% and a productivity growing 2% per year (0%) since 1994. The World Bank diagnosis lies on three pillars: growth, competitiveness, and the role of the State. Productivity will grow thanks to genuine or imitated innovation and an effectiveness using of production factors. For the World Bank, the obstacles to productivity are: - The high cost of labour; - a less efficient vocational system that undermines the workers' training effectiveness; - The high cost of connectivity to Internet; - the weaknesses of the corporation in charge of standardization, and the difficulty to get an ISO certification; - an underdeveloped financial sector with banks refractory to risks taking, that limits the access to financing for SMEs; - bureaucracy and administrative heaviness that directly undermine enterprises' productivity. As private sector and households save only 13% of their revenue (32.7% in Nigeria), Cameroon has to massively mobilize the Foreign Direct Investment (FDI). The second pillar, competition, is confined at the national level: - the State participation and subsidies to enterprises limits rivalry among enterprises; - the price control also limits imports and exacerbates markets concentration.

The availability of an effective transportation infrastructure, in a broader perspective also of a robust communication infrastructure and access to efficient utility providers for electricity, water, and so on has long been noticed as an important influence on productivity and competitiveness: The distribution of firm productivity is likely driven by other factors, especially the context for strategy and rivalry,

The social infrastructure and political institutions that slowly changed in Cameroon over time have an important impact on long-term prosperity levels. Government has influence on factors at all levels.

To better understand Cameroon's strategic positioning, a brief examination of some industrial models will permit to have an idea of approaches experimented to challenge the obstacles of an underdeveloped country.

1. UNLOCK GLOBAL COMPETITIVENESS FORCES OF CAMEROON'S ECONOMY

The Cameroon economy globally relies on agriculture and the export of raw materials. The major overall objective is to achieve a sustained GDP growth rate of at least 10% over a decade, marked by a broad diversification of sources of wealth creation, a more dense and complex integration of the various branches of activity with an increasing effect of products from manufacturing industry (about 25% of GDP) and a substantial increase in exports of goods from manufacturing industry (about 50% of total exports), and the development of a financial industry capable of mobilizing the necessary resources internally and internationally (particularly FDI). The challenge of this industrialization dynamics is to make Cameroon the "Factory of the New Industrial Africa"; that's why the competitiveness of the Cameroon's economy is a great challenge.

The WEF's Global Competitiveness Report (WEF, GCR, 2011, pp. 4-10) features 12 pillars for competitiveness: Institutions; Infrastructure; Macroeconomic Environment; Health and Primary Education; Higher Education and Training; Goods Market Efficiency; Labour Market Efficiency; Financial Market Development; Technological Readiness; Market Size; Business Sophistication; Innovation. The Cameroon Economy Profile from the Global Competitiveness Report 2018 features various indicators. Its rank: 121st over 140 countries of the inquiry is not a good indication announcing the Cameroon's candidature for emergence.

The way Cameroon is striving to follow since years is industrialization in imitating policies formulated in different countries and in different contexts.

1.1. PROTO-INDUSTRIAL CAMEROON AND FREE TRADE

The free trade regime has been practiced systematically since the end of the 19th century under the "Open Door Regime" in German Cameroon. The country had thus opted for an all-round economic liberalism, an orientation considered as the first paradigm in the construction of its industry and trade. Cameroon exported palm kernel and wood productions intensively to Germany until 1933, and Germany in turn sold cement, machinery and beer to Cameroon. The Netherlands bought cocoa and oilseeds from Cameroon. France, as a sales representative (traveller-resident-placer), was in charge of negotiating new export markets for Cameroon products. From France, Cameroon imported wines, liqueurs, stationery, metals and clothing. Cameroon bought mainly from Great Britain, coal, cement, irons, steel and cotton, while it depended on the United States for wheat flour, leaf tobacco, petrol and oil. As early as 1935, the United States bought Cameroonian wood, palm oil and sesame, while porcelain, earthenware, crystal glasses, bicycles, tyres and canned food arrived Cameroon from Japan.

The oldest of the consular chambers, the Cameroon Chamber of Commerce, Industry, Mines and Handicrafts (CCIMA), was set up in 1911. It is a public consultative body representing the interests of the private business community, including those of service providers.

At the corporate level, the *Syndicat des Industriels du Cameroun* (SYDUSTRICAM) was created in 1950 to defend the interests of promoters before the public authorities and maintain a dialogue with the workers' unions. The current Cameroon Employers Association (GICAM) was created in 1957 and was then called

Groupement Interprofessionnel pour l'Etude et la Coordination des Intérêts Economiques.

These organizations, which are in a way gentlemen's clubs, often remained transparent and their influence on industrial affairs were not always known to the general public, with the exception of the renewal periods of their executives.

In terms of business creation, the oldest of the companies registered in the distribution sector is probably RW KING, created in Bristol, Great Britain, which moved to Douala in 1930. It trades and guarantees the after-sales service of the products and brands it represents. This company is still firmly established in Cameroon; it is far from being an endangered species despite its age.

At the strategic level, the consequences of the economic crisis that broke out in the United States in 1929 were felt in Cameroon from 1930 and 1931. Incentive measures were implemented for the resumption of coffee, rubber, banana and oilseed production, whose falling prices were weighing heavily on the will power of producers whose standard of living had been severely eroded. The British mandate administration created the CDC (Cameroon Development Corporation) in 1947, rehabilitating private German plantations on the slopes of Mount Cameroon. It also organized farmers to produce the same products that the CDC bought back for processing or export.

According to G. COURADE, "the state bureaucracy believed that the archaic local peasantry was technically incapable of achieving the necessary diversification and increasing agricultural production[1]". Thus, the integration of peasants into the capitalist movement which Cameroon

---

[1]. Courade G. Expensive farms; the agro-industrial priority of Cameroonian agriculture)". Politique Africaine 14, June 1984, pp75-79.

had opted for was constantly postponed because of prejudices about their ability to assimilate doctrines and modes of production. The preference was to employ them as low-paid workers because of their low degree of emancipation.

Things did not change after the country's independence; and G. COURADE exclaimed indignantly: "the post-colonial Cameroonian State has preferred to make agricultural development dependent on a few costly agro-industrial complexes, rather than a multitude of family farms.[2]". This last option will only be rehabilitated at the beginning of 2010, and will become the core of the Second Generation Agricultural Policy.

The Brasseries du Cameroun, another flagship of pre-independence creations, has undergone very significant development since 1948, its year of birth, to the point of occupying the position of invincible leader by new entrants in a highly competitive beverage sector. Several of its rivals had to file for bankruptcy, overtaken by the subtleties of the marketing mix, the shock of the penetration and control of the large market and niches.

ALUCAM (Aluminium du Cameroun), a semi-public company, moved to the Sanaga industrial basin in 1954, as part of a partnership with the French group Pechiney. This company, which began its processing activities with alumina imported from Guinea Conakry, soon catalysed the country's hopes in the field of heavy industry. It had a high potential for expansion and many opportunities for subcontracting; but its capacities will for long remain under-exploited due to a low supply of electrical energy.

Important note: Companies created before independence have gone through the most delicate phases of their life

---

[2] . Ditto

cycle, and are fully mature at the beginning of the 21st century. This solidity results from a combination of strategic complementarities between Cameroon; host country and shareholder; and transnational groups jealous of the sustainability and profitability of their global operations. They erected barriers when leaving their field of activity by increasing the volume of tangible investments. When the energy equation will be resolved, these companies will undoubtedly find new youthfulness and dynamism to conquer markets that have remained beyond their reach until now.

1.2. THE INDUSTRIAL STRATEGY OF CAMEROON UNDER FRENCH SUPERVISION

In the aftermath of the Second World War, the tutelary power opted for an economic take-off based on Development Plans. From 1946 to 1960, two Quadrennial Plans (qp) were adopted with objectives whose implementation was considered satisfactory.

The First Quadrennial Plan (Qp1) was experimented from 1946 – 1950. 85% of the allocations in this plan (Qp1) were devoted to infrastructure, whose number of projects could be counted on the fingers of one hand:

i. the development of the Douala sea port;
ii. the improvement of the railways;
iii. the construction of earth roads;
iv. the construction of aerodromes;
v. The acquisition of modern means of transmission.

The Second Quadrennial Plan (Qp2): 1956-1960

This was devoted to the completion of major infrastructure works which started during the Qp1 but also, through the development of agricultural production (40% of the voted appropriations, i.e. 10 times more than during

Qp1). To achieve the major objective of increasing the living standards of the population, half a dozen strategies were adopted, three of which were related to industrialization. These included:

1°) Diversification and enhancement of agricultural wealth (production of selected high-yielding species, training of a farmer through the supervision of agents from rural modernization sectors);

2°) Training and development of human capital;

3°) Educating the producer.

Both of these four-year plans were financed to the tune of CFAF 96 billion, thanks to French public and semi-public funds (CFAF 65 billion, or 68%); CFAF 10 billion was drawn from the Cameroonian State and Municipal budgets; CFAF 21 billion from private funding.

In view of the positive results generated by the four-year plan, general guidelines were assigned to the 1st Five-Year Development Plan.

2. THE INDEPENDENT CAMEROON AND THE GENESIS OF INDUSTRIALIZATION

Cameroon and Industrialization Models[3]

Economic analysis distinguishes three main models of industrialization:

- Industrializing industries;
- Industrialization by import substitution
- Industrialization by export promotion

[3] . Thomas Coutrot & Michel Husson (1993): "*The Destinies of Third World Countries; Assessment, Report and prospects*"; under the supervision of C-D Echaudemaison. Published at Editions Nathan.

This classification is not exclusive and often has combinations or a strategic mix depending on the countries and circumstances. Nevertheless, the late industrialization countries in Asia, Latin America and Africa experimented with industrialization through import substitution, but with totally different results. While Asian countries got away with it, Africans failed woefully. The Latinos maintained an intermediate position from these two extremes. Asian countries have also excelled in the model of industrialization by promoting exports, which South Korea has championed; hence the name: Korean model.

In 1960, the year of its independence, Cameroon drew up its first Five-Year Development Plan (FYP), which it adopted the following year; it covered the period 1961-1966.

The morphology of the economy at the beginning of FYP1 presents:

- a relatively low population density and a moderate population growth rate;
- a very favourable but insufficiently developed agricultural and livestock production potential, with overall food consumption at the limit of needs;
- an embryonic manufacturing industry;
- an infrastructure of developing means of communication;
- very rudimentary domestic trade channels;
- a national per capita income of 21,500 CFA francs on average, comparable to that of other countries in the inter-tropical zone of America and Asia;
- Balanced public finances and trade balance thanks to very substantial external assistance.

Industrialization Based on Agriculture

Cameroon's industrial process began long before independence, but it is established that agriculture existed at the beginning. Commenting on this issue, René Dumont said: "We advised some priorities to industrial development. Without factories, there can be no possible take-off of the economy, no rapid increase in labour productivity, no supply of modern means of production in agriculture. Industrialization also guarantees some dignity achieved in the economic order[4]".

The progress made in the sector of agriculture from Cameroon's first industrialization was promising despite the low density of the road network, and the lack of a conducive means of transport for the movement of people and food. Extensive polyculture of cereals, legumes and tubers is practiced throughout the country and its product sold on periodic markets with low monetization, where barter was still the dominant means of exchange.

The French administration organized indigenous cooperatives to boost the production of export crops: cocoa, Arabica and Robusta coffee, bananas, cotton, oil palm, tobacco, rubber, tea and bananas. These cash crops are expanding rapidly and occupy a 90% of the rural population. Teaching of agriculture was provided in farm-schools and experimental gardens. Agricultural school mutual served as educational tools and incubators for small agro-pastoral projects.

All this supervision sometimes came up against very heavy rural conservatism that protected the customs and eating habits of the populations.

---

[4] Dumont René, "False Start in Africa" (1962); Le Seuil; Edition revised and corrected in 1973; page 100.

The State also created integrated societies for the development and management of agricultural basins, while an oligarchy of physiocrats was involved in the cultivation of coffee, cape tobacco and cotton.

Food Industries

The annual need for flour consumed in Cameroon was 160,000 quintals in 1961. This figure will reach 200,000 quintals five years later. The installation of flour mills was therefore possible considering imports from Chad (19,000 quintals) and the Central African Republic (16,500 quintals) that were transiting through Douala. An economic study for the manufacture of biscuits was also carried out. The conclusion was in favour of import substitution, but on condition that domestic demand reaches the break-even point of 400 tons per year. However, since Cameroon's biscuit consumption in 1960 was only 150 tons, this project was also abandoned without taking into account the evolution of demand and Chadian and Central African imports of 120 tons from each country.

This means that Cameroon has not always had the last word on the decision to locate industrial units on its territory; rather, it is the holders of capital and technology who bear this responsibility.

Textile Industries

Cotton cultivation was introduced in Cameroon in the 1940s. Cotton production for the 1958-1959 season was 22,000 tons giving 7,575 tons of fibres cotton and 344 tons of yellow cotton. It is this availability of raw materials that made it possible to set up a spinning and weaving plant in Douala, whose profitability was only possible if the public authorities agreed to ensure the training of the needed personnel, and grant financial facilities and tax breaks during the break-in period. The prices of factors of production such as water and electricity were also to be subsidized. This factory had to use 1,000 tons of cotton per year at start up to produce blankets. But the creation of this blanket production unit was unable to withstand the argument of an import cost price that was CFAF 252,965, compared to CFAF 335,650 per ton produced locally. This decision was thus made in without taking cognizance of the knock-on effects, the income multiplier effect, the learning effect, and the experience curve related to the territorial establishment of a plant.

2.1. THE FIRST IMPORT/SUBSTITUTION MODEL

The vision of industrial development commissioned by the Government of Cameroon was the subject of a call for proposals submitted to the *Société d'Etudes pour le Développement Economique et Social* (S.E.D.E.S). Conclusions of this study over determined Cameroon's industrial prospects and patterns, selecting the companies to be created, and the costs associated with the identified investments. It was in fact at that moment that the first paradigm shift occurred, corresponding to the transition from an open-door or free trade regime to an import substitution regime marked by the protection of infant industries. The Cameroonian economic area thus became a market sheltered by discriminatory or researcher-headed external tariffs.

This tension immediately led to the erection of trade barriers and the setting of prices for essential goods by the administration. In other words, it was the instrumentation of protectionism that was being put in place, causing distortions and rigidities which impacted the behaviour of economic agents for decades to come. Shielded by customs barriers, companies that establish themselves in a quasi-monopoly situation struggle to structure their national or sub-regional expansion.

Insufficient local savings and domestic demand resulted in low investment. The preference for self-financing by many small firms showed the reluctance of annuitants who prefer investment security to industrial risks.

The strategy adopted ended up consisting in protecting entire industrial sectors from competition:

- energy;
- mineral products;
- wood;
- textiles;
- food processing;
- Various industries.

Thus, in the absence of economic intelligence initiatives and due to dependence on external technologies and inputs for industry and, also the importation of technicians and engineers, the delay in Cameroon's industrialization became inevitable.

2.2. PRODUCTION LIMITS IMPOSED ON INDUSTRIES BY INSUFFICIENT ENERGY

In 1960, the *Société Camerounaise des Laminoirs* (SOCALAM) was founded as an extension of the tanks of the *Société d'Aluminium du Cameroun* (ALUCAM), created in 1954 and specialized in the manufacture of sheet metal. It contributed to the expansion of an industrial complex that had just welcomed ALUBASSA, a company that manufactured household items among other things. A double constraint will permanently handicap the anticipated progress of downstream industrialization in the aluminium sector, and deprive the economy of competitiveness and growth drivers which would have pulled other sectors such as non-ferrous metals and chemicals. These were: the import of alumina from Conakry (Guinea) and the low supply of electricity. The phenomenon persisted and was likely to continue due to inadequate investment in relation to general economic development and population growth.

Table 1: Creations of enterprises between 1960 and 1965

No.	COMPANY	Share capital in millions F CFA	Field of activity	Number of employees
1	SOSUCAM	200	SUGAR	1,342
2	CHOCOCAM	652	CHOCOLATE	362
3	CICAM	2,137	Textile	1,615
4	ENAC	20	Textile	75
5	BATA	885	Shoes	821
6	SACC	450	Shoes	200
7	EFC	200	Wood	180
8	FORESTIERE CAMPO	200	Wood	150
9	CEP	223	Chemistry	82
10	SIPCA	300	Perfume industry	124
11	EE	425	Electronics	200
12	SOPARCA	60	Perfume industry	104
13	PLASTICAM	585	Plastic	272
14	SAFACAM	1,820	Rubber	2,200
15	MAVEM	80	Plastic	152
16	CIMENCAM	2,800	Cement	624
17	SCBM	40	Concrete	50
18	UIC	500	Mechanics	150
19	TROPIC	450	Mechanics	150
20	CTMC	210	Mechanics	150
21	SCI	100	Mechanics	120
TOTAL		14,030		9,129

Source: industrial file of SYNDUSTRICAM.

2.3. INDUSTRIALIZATION SUPPORTING INSTRUMENTS

As concerns instruments to support industries development, the Cameroon Development Bank (CDB) and the National Investment Corporation (SNI) has helped to acquire a mechanism to fund the fragile industrial and commercial process. The CDB provided business credits to individuals and companies, as well as medium- and long-term investment credits. The SNI managed the State's portfolio of assets in the semi-public sector and in semi-public companies. Four other institutions were created in the 1970s: the Assistance Centre for the Promotion of Small and Medium-sized Enterprises (CAPME, 1970); the Industrial Zone Management and Development Authority (MAGZI, 1971); the Assistance and Guarantee Fund for Small and MEDIUM-sized Enterprises (FOGAPE, 1975) and the National Foreign Trade Centre (CNCE, 1979). On the legal level, an Investment Code for Eastern Cameroon was the subject of Law No. 60-64 of 27 June 1960; it included the first guidelines of the industrial policy based on import substitution as well as the associated incentives.

2.4. PROGRESS AND SETBACKS IN THE FIRST PHASE OF INDUSTRIALIZATION

The food and textile industries were the first two driving industries in the transition from a cottage industry to an industrial economy. The textile industry systematically imported French machines, techniques and technicians. Its development was much slower due to a weak societal base. The food industry was met with shortcomings in the supply of raw materials from subsistence farming using rudimentary tools. On the other hand, the steel industry was unable to get off the ground due to the lack of development of the identified iron deposits, the isolation of the mining basins and inadequate electrical energy supply. At the scientific and technical level, the creation of high schools (the National School of Administration and Magistracy, the Higher Teachers Training College, National School of

Agronomy) was part of the training of local human resources for development.

Secondary and higher education were initially reserved for a small number of young people recruited from the periphery of traditional chiefdoms (school was initially seen as another version of slavery). The supply of qualified engineers and technicians did not therefore keep pace with demand. Although the training of senior managers was more visible in agriculture, most graduates were integrated as civil servants in the public administration and assigned to open positions at national, sector-based or territorial level. A few privileged people benefited from appointments as CEO (Chief Executive Officer) or DG (Director General) to manage State agricultural, pastoral or fisheries projects. They were thus converted into managers or administrators/managers, disconnecting them from their academic profile.

At the ideological level, Cameroon made its choice from the first Five-Year Program (FYP-1) onwards to manage its economy on a doctrinal basis called **Planned Liberalism**, a **State Capitalism** in fact.

3. INDUSTRIAL POLICY AT THE 2nd FIVE-YEAR PROGRAMME (FYP-2):1966-1971

Analysis of the factors and conditions of industrial development revealed significant changes and the existence of some constraints and assets. The assets identified included among others:

- the potential for exploiting hydroelectric and gas resources;
- a road, rail and port infrastructure network under development, although user fees are still high;
- a large and fairly skilled workforce;

- the rapidly expanding though poorly organized urban craft industry;
- a dynamic private sector and diversified industrial activities;
- A structured public administration with a nationwide presence.

Constraints were also present and included:

- the high cost of investments related to the location of industrial projects based on energy and transport infrastructure;
- a limited level of qualification in high-tech jobs;
- the sizing of the factories according to open markets;
- the overall high interest rates on loans;
- Undeveloped mining and energy resources.

3.1. THE SHIFT IN INDUSTRIALIZATION BASED ON AGRICULTURE

With 47% of value added from the primary sector, Cameroon in the second five-year programme relief leaned on **"Agricultural Industries"** to build its manufacturing sector. The objectives set for the medium and long term were as follows:

- crop diversification;
- substitution of local products for imported consumer goods;
- maximum on-site processing of local products;
- Penetration of domestic and regional markets and control prices.

But these initiatives did not prosper at all, due to strategic weakness; hence the setting of production targeted for "Agricultural Industries", according to the table below.

Table 2: Investments in "Agricultural industries" (in millions of CFA francs)

ITEM	COST		ANNUAL DISTRIBUTION				
	Total	2nd Program	I	II	III	IV	V
Robusta coffee	125	125	-	-	-	50	75
Arabica coffee	175	175	50	55		35	35
Palm oil	1,343	624	6	56	7	200	355
Tea	271	166	13	11	36	10	96
Cotton	150	150	-	70		80	-
Latex processing	236	130	24	29	24	24	29
Rice	110	110	-	50	60	-	-
Cocoa-butter-mass	601	501	235	161	35	35	35
CREATIONS							
Industrial sugar only	1,360	1,360	960	400	-	-	-
Tomato concentrate	40	40	-	-	-	-	40
Pineapple - slices - juice	100	100	-	-	-	100	-
Perfume plants	25	25	-	15	-	10	-
Studies	70	70	-	-	20	20	30
RENEWAL		3,576	1,288	847	182	564	695
TOTAL		1,480	250	270	290	320	350
TOTAL INVESTMENTS		5,056	1,538	1,117	472	884	1,045

Source: Ministry of Programming and Regional Development

Food Industries were undergoing significant expansion and diversification, with industrial bakeries (90% of sector-base production in 1963/1964) and industrial slaughterhouses. Ground coffee, pasta, chocolate, candies, canned beef, wheat flour were then manufactured from industrial facilities based in Douala. Livestock feeds, cookies and frozen shrimps and prawns were part of this category of projects that were doing well. Similarly, industrial fishing could make it possible to obtain canned fish and fishmeal.

Table 3: Investments in "Food Industries" (cost in millions of CFA francs)

TYPE OF OPERATION	COST		ANNUAL DISTRIBUTION				
	Total	2nd Program	I	II	III	IV	V
Chocolates - candies	250	200	150	50	-	-	-
Canned beef	46	5	5	-	-	-	-
Wheat flour - derivatives	375	375	300	75	-	-	-
Biscuits	17	17	-	-	-	17	-
Frozen shrimps and prawns	25	25	-	25	-	-	-
Instant coffee	400	400	-	-	100	200	100
Studies	75	75	15	15	15	15	15
TOTAL		1,097	470	165	115	232	115
RENEWAL		765	110	130	150	175	200
TOTAL INVESTMENTS	1,188	1,862	580	295	265	407	315

Source: Ministry of Programming and Regional Development

Table 4: Business start-ups from 1965 to 1970; capital in millions F CFA

N°	COMPANY	SHARE CAPITAL	FIELD OF ACTIVITY	NUMBER OF EMPLOYEES
1	SOCAPALM	11,400	Palm oil	4,921
2	PAMOL	1,400	Palm oil	2,843
3	SCM	736	Flour milling	173
4	GUINESS	1,920	Brewery	1,376
5	UCB	800	Brewery	426
6	SYNTHECAM	200	Textile	149
7	SIVA	50	Textile	97
8	SOCATEX	240	Textile	125
9	DRATEX	60	Textile	100
10	SICABO	15	Textile	200
11	SNC BOIS	160	Wood	300
12	COCAM	510	Wood	455
13	SCEFL	65	Chemistry	17
14	SCIMPOS	51	Chemistry	51
15	CAMOA	276	Chemistry	55
16	PILCAM	1,000	Chemistry	277
17	SOCAVER	1,100	Chemistry	219
18	CERICAM	1,200	Ceramic	218
19	SOLADO	1,475	Metalworking industry	162
20	SOCOMECAM	250	Metalworking industry	80
21	SOCADEM	160	Metalworking industry	50
22	ENA	100	Metalworking industry	100
23	SATC	100	Metalworking industry	200
24	SAFCA	400	Paper	100
TOTAL		23,423		12,594

Source: SYNDUSTRICAM's industrial file

In addition to Agricultural Industries, Building Materials Industries were emerging and experiencing real development. The productions identified were: lime, bricks, agglomerated tiles, manufactured concrete.

Building Materials and Wood Industries

Producing cement by a monopoly, CIMENCAM aimed to meet the growing demand from construction companies and households. This cement was also exported to Chad. The prices charged by CIMENCAM were considered inflationary, hence the periodic tax revisions. Wood production, processing and marketing was subject to programming that contrasts with the trial and error observed during FYP-1.

The following table provides a measure of the importance of activity in this sector.

Table 5: Investments in "Wood Industries" (In millions of CFA francs)

ITEM	COST		ANNUAL DISTRIBUTION				
	Total	2nd Program	I	II	III	IV	V
Sawing	967	827	88	221	226	92	200
Unrolling - plywood - slats	1,250	975	160	140	120	280	275
Carpentry and cabinetmaking work	150	150	24	24	24	37	41
Mosaic floor	50	50	-	25	25	-	-
Studies on "Wood processing industry"	15	15	15	-	-	-	-
TOTAL		2,017	287	410	395	409	516
RENEWAL		305	45	50	60	70	80
TOTAL INVESTMENTS	2,432	2,322	332	460	455	479	596

Source: Ministry of Programming and Regional Development

Industries for Shoes – Textiles -Clothing

The dynamism in this rapidly changing sector was impressive: 86% of the planned investments were made during this FYP-2.

Table 6: Investments in "Textile Industries" (in millions of CFA francs)

ITEM	COST		ANNUAL DISTRIBUTION				
	Total	2nd Program	I	II	III	IV	V
Manufacturing		150	-	-	-	50	100
Shoes	320	320	-	150	100	70	-
Hosiery	135	60	-	-	10	40	10
Unbleached and finished cotton fabrics	2,370	920	-	-	250	420	250
Blankets	173	173	-	50	100	23	-
Sacks manufacturing	400	400	-	-	100	250	50
Miscellaneous	158	125	-	-	-	-	125
Studies		8	6	2	-	-	-
TOTAL		2,156	6	202	560	853	535
RENEWAL		895	125	150	175	205	240
TOTAL INVESTMENTS	3,556	3,051	131	352	735	1,058	775

Source: Ministry of Programming and Regional Development

This sector could have become a driving force behind the country's industrialization at the time when the Cameroon Cotton Development Corporation (SODECOTON) began producing the necessary raw material. Unfortunately, the planned investments were not implemented with the desired efficiency. Moreover, international competition from fabrics subjected to economic and social dumping and the flooding of the national market by second-hand clothing from mafia networks were factors that had worsen competition.

Visibily,Cameroon had not been a State of strategist neither in diversification nor in specialization and even less in niches; did it lose the war through its refusal to fight and its state of resignation even though it still had strong competitive arguments?

The "Aluminium" Industry

Since its creation in 1954, ALUCAM has been the country's largest industrial project. However, its development was severely disrupted 10 years later due to insufficient electricity supply, particularly during the low water level at the Edea dam.

Indeed, the Cameroonian industry had faced energy deficits after its independence. Demand increased over the course of the country's industrial history yet appropriate solutions were not implemented. The opening of the Minim Martap bauxite mine was postponed due to the lack of hydroelectric and rail networks. Hence, visibly,Cameroon remained dependent on Conakry's bauxite imports for a long time, and ALUCAM operated below its optimum even after the solution to the energy equation.

Mechanical and Electrical Industries

The main activities of this branch consisted of repairs on machinery and motor vehicles (74%); the remaining 26% were divided into: various metal constructions (blacksmithing, carpentry, boiler making, etc.), manufacture of nails, grills, furniture and metal canteens, bicycles, installations and repair of electrical equipment. The manufacture of handling and transport equipment, mopeds, trailers, tools and agricultural machinery were also included.

The installation of transistor receivers and radio equipment was one of the achievements indicating progress towards technological mastery.

CONCLUSION OF FYP-2

Industrial development during the second five-year plan was characterized by the mobilization of all social components to improve monetary income in both urban and rural areas. This objective of social justice and strategic coherence was accompanied by other economic and financial management measures, including:

- The development of international opportunities;
- Dialogue between the administrative and private spheres to improve the business climate;
- Negotiations with development partners to strengthen fiscal discipline, mobilize domestic savings and increase external assistance;
- The participation of all stakeholders in the implementation of the development plan and the adaptation of State intervention to the requirements of the productive sector;
- Information to beneficiaries;
- Rigorous control and follow-up of public funds, including development aid and local authority finances;
- Great increase in the effort to rationalize human capital in order to increase its ability to contribute to productive efficiency.

On the financial level, the Cameroon Development Bank (CDB) applied the selective credit policy towards the productive investments also selected. The control of administered prices was systematic in this context of low competition where even imports were monitored, regulated or quota-controlled.

With the prospect of developing new mineral and forest resources, and the guarantee of a controlled macroeconomic framework, Cameroon was surely moving towards its economic take-off; it is this challenge that the 1970s eventually took on.

3.2. THIRD FIVE-YEAR PROGRAMME INDUSTRIAL POLICY

Cameroon's industrial policy was without surprise, oriented towards the transformation of local agricultural, pastoral, forestry, and mining and energy resources. It was complemented by the development of transport, the extension of transport infrastructure, trade diversification, intermediate consumption products and processing industries for final consumption.

The macroeconomic indicators at the beginning of FYP-3 heralded a new era with:

- an equipment budget growing at a rate of 25% per year;
- the acceleration of industrial expansion;
- an annual population growth rate of 2.1%;
- a GDP growth rate of 9.8%;
- a monetary depreciation rate of 3.5%;
- a strong production from companies in the agro-food sector.

The young companies that were expected to expand very strongly were concentrated in cotton weaving and plastic articles. The Cameroon Sugar Company (SOSUCAM) was set up in 1974 thanks to a partnership between the State of Cameroon and the J.L., VILGRAIN and SOMDIAA French Groups.

Industrial Production Objectives of Fyp-3

The value added of secondary sector activities was expected to more than double, from CFAF 45 billion in

1967-1968 to CFAF 91.5 billion in 1975-1976, representing an average annual growth rate of 10.8%. This sector performance was driven by a small number of industrial sectors with very high growth rates:

Table 7: Industrial growth rate by industry sector

1) Textile; leather; shoes	20.5%
2) Mechanical and electrical engineering; wood	17.8%
3) Building material; ores; aluminium; chemistry	16.6%
4) Food industries	15.8%
5) Beverages; tobacco	10.2%

Author's calculations based on raw data of FYP-3.

Cameroon intended to rebuild its industrialization on the development of mining resources whose reserves had already been identified and estimated. This was once more a lost hope. Nevertheless, we were witnessing the resetting of the expectations formulated during the two previous FYP- that led to a deadlock. And yet, as the saying goes: "**if the music changes, let's also change the dance step".** Of course, since the music doesn't change, we can guess what happens next.

The so-called "transformation" activities announced in this second phase of industrialization benefitted from protection and encouragement measures taken by public authorities within the framework of regional or international agreements. Aluminium production still continued, but with results below potential. Its downstream integration remained limited, as in the past, by a critical supply of electrical energy. All in all, the growth of metallurgy and the development of mining resources were still hampered by the very high cost of operating processes, the isolation of mining basins and the absence of local SMIs/SMEs specializing in the outsourcing of mining products.

The primary processing industries for agricultural products evolved in line with the small surpluses generated by household consumption. Shortages and discontinuities in the supply of raw materials for long hindered the development of the agro-food industry.

3.4. POLICY OF SUPPORT TO STRENGTHEN THE SMEs/ SMIs

The emergence and consolidation of a network of SMEs was supported by an organization created in 1970, the *Centre d'Assistance aux Petites et Moyennes Entreprises* (CAPME). This institution, which is at the heart of the technical support system, had a wide range of skills. More precisely, it was charged with:

- Identifying projects, assisting their promoters throughout the investment and operating process of the company;
- Conducting market and feasibility studies, partner search, product selection, business strategy, costing;
- Ensuring the creative process: design, choice of equipment and manufacturing processes, industrial design, reliability tests, equipment maintenance, etc.;
- Configuring accounting, inventory and personnel management, financial diagnosis, profitability study;
- Planning the training of business leaders and the professional development of staff.

The planning activity that was missing from CAPME's missions were integrated into FOGAPE (*Fonds d'Aide et de Garantie aux Petites et Moyennes Entreprises*). This structure was therefore created to provide financial support to SMEs; and bound to:

- Provide guarantees for credits granted to SMEs;
- Take stakes in the capital of SMEs or directly grant equity loans;

- Contribute to the conduct of studies on projects of interest to SMEs;
- Provide assistance in training, information, advice and accounting.

But despite its high degree of solicitation and usefulness, CAPME was sacrificed on the altar of the crisis on the pretext of the structural reforms proposed by the IMF and the World Bank. Through this, they had "**thrown out the baby with the bathwater**".

The FYP-3 was also leaned on two levers:

- The competitiveness of competing companies in regional markets; and
- The competitiveness of public authorities called upon to convince investors, by creating an incentive environment.

This is how the long-term vision of industrial policy began to emerge. From this point on, the system's strategists turned their attention to international markets to seek partners and opportunities. **Export Promotion Industrialization** (EPI) was thus adopted, even without proclaiming it, to complement **Industrialization by Import Substitution** (ISI). Three essential factors could make it possible to achieve this strategic mix in the long term:

1°) the enormous potentialities in natural, human and financial resources, as well as the possibilities offered by the industrial equipment and infrastructure acquired or planned;

2°) the growing and diversified demand for finished or semi-finished products for domestic or industrial use likely to be manufactured in Cameroon;

3°) The collaboration with African countries having comparable industrial level, and facing the same problems, for a concerted search for exit routes.

From then on, a leap forward became likely, but once again under constraints of:

- the production of sufficient energy in quantity and at attractive rates;
- The increasing valorisation of primary products.

Table 8: Exports of the main products

DESIGNATION	1963 / 1964		1970 / 1971		Index in value
	Quantity (tons)	Value (million F)	Quantity (tons)	Value (million F)	
Products from agricultural industries					
Robusta coffee	34,500	4,968	59,000	8,673	175
Arabica coffee	13,230	2,593	19,000	4,161	160
Palm oil	10,200	561	15,000	765	136
Tea	316	76	930	233	307
Cotton fibre	15,920	2,181	26,200	3,589	165
Rubber	9,110	1,057	16,800	1,949	184
Cocoa mass	6,000	144	11,550	277	192
Products from other industries					
Cement			18,000	340	
Chocolates- candies			1,410	592	
Sawn wood (m^3)	16,764	285	25,000	425	149
Peeled timber	20,593	216	34,600	363	168
Plywood - Lathed			31,300	1,565	
Aluminium	43,000	4,515	52,000	5,460	121
Cotton oil	900	57	1,650	104	182
Peanut oil			3,200	350	
Perfume industry	100	33	800	260	788

Source: Ministry of Programs and Regional Development/SOPECAM,

Table 9: Evolution of production of the main crops (in tons)

CULTURES	YEAR				
	2004	2005	2006	2007	2008
Cotton	306,000	208,000	184,000	179,149	111,468
Cocoa	158,826	182,959	191,590	212,619	229,203
Coffee	56,265	43,859	45,622	47,792	50,687
Rubber	54,523	58,689	61,736	46,807	53,477
Pineapple	48,424	100,319	106,349	116,710	127,070
Sweet bananas	797,739	929,950	969,967	1,024, 004	1,078, 041
Plantain	1,314,898	2,012, 548	2,175, 434	2,338, 036	2,500, 639
Beans/niebe	199,868	234,218	248,180	259,411	270,642
Peanut	225,720	346,448	414,046	449,123	484,199
Palm oil	172,047	198,325	205,318	215,462	225,606
Yam	286,494	343,270	366,808	383,212	399,615
Sweet potatoes	190,071	206,477	221,342	211,037	235,728
Maize	966,106	1,050, 396	1,249, 489	1,322, 160	1,394, 832
Millet/sorghum	607,814	828,832	917,107	977,250	1,023,327
Cassava	2,092,763	2,393, 801	2,652, 176	2,767, 455	2,882, 734
Irish potatoes	142,407	133,811	142,118	143,568	145,018
Rained rice	49,958	58,369	64,525	68,267	72,009
Tomatoes	408,064	488,790	522,251	548,418	572,219

Source: DESA/MINADER, 2010.

Apart from the export of semi-processed agricultural products, the five-year period was marked by an increase in the diversity of products from other industries. There was a significant evolution in cotton-based products, particularly fabrics, clothing and hosiery. The export of aluminium corrugated and rolled sheets increased significantly. The identification of the possibilities for setting up new industrial units was completed, in particular for:

- the manufacture of semi-finished products and the supply of intermediate goods or finished products to external markets;
- the assembly and finishing of complex components in high-tech industries;
- research by public authorities or in association with private companies, into export markets within the framework of the ACP-EEC agreements;
- the gradual anchoring of industry in the economy: inter-company, inter-branch and inter-sectorial exchanges, local savings geared towards industrial investments, the diversification of vocational training in industrial trades;
- The development of industrial zones to facilitate the establishment of foreign developers and the removal of uncertainty regarding the viability of industrial sites.

It is in this context that MAGZI (Industrial Zone Management and Development Authority) was created in 1971. In the same package of measures, creation of a Project Design Office was envisaged at MINDIC (Ministry of Industrial and Commercial Development).

This structure was responsible for analysing the economic, financial and technological aspects of industrial projects. Market and feasibility studies had become systematic to accompany each application for approval to finance a project. This approach later became mechanical and led to the identical reproduction of the studies without regard to the specificities inherent in the company's leadership, management and environment. However, these expert reports enabled the State to measure the social and economic interest of the proposed industrial projects for the country. They were also a useful tool for industrial promotion and provided interested entrepreneurs with information for assessing risk and the anticipated profitability of investments.

Even diplomacy came to the rescue of the industry. The State created economic missions in Europe and North America, forgetting the emerging countries of Asia or Latin America with which the gaps in industrial performance were smaller and likely to facilitate complementarities of knowledge and experience. Moreover, the contribution of these missions to industrial promotion has never been evaluated. With hindsight, it turns out that these were prestigious creations, which were budget-consuming and without a real vision.

CONCLUSION

As with the FYP-2 industrial forecasts, those included in the FYP-3 would have had difficulty coming true despite the renewed enthusiasm thanks to the strategic review that catalysed the shift towards Industrialization through Export Promotion.

Energy stress continued to demotivate industrial players. It was aggravated by the rise in oil prices caused by the October 1973 Yom Kippur War. The crisis thus created, increasing the oil bill only worsened the chronic energy deficit and aggravated the gaps in project implementation through the increase in the cost of imported inputs for industry.

4. THE FOURTH FIVE-YEAR DEVELOPMENT PROGRAMME (FYP-4): 1976 – 1981

The Irresistible Slowdown

The diagnosis made by the planning engineer at the beginning of the FYP-4 is uncompromising: Industrial development was slowing down despite its potential, for good reasons:

- insufficient energy production;
- poor integration of the industrial sector into the economy;
- lack of information, promotion and incentives for industrial decentralization;
- insufficient contribution of local private savings to the industrial sector;
- insufficient transfer of capital in the industrial sector;
- Low competitiveness of existing industries, which itself results from designing and sizing of companies.

For the six diagnosed diseases, some chronic or inherited, and others emerging, several therapies have been considered, including those already tested in previous FYPs. The new prescription includes four items:

- Production of heavy equipment for the consumption of intermediate goods industries;
- Promotion of modern craftsmanship;
- Promotion of Cameroon capital-intensive industrial activities and managers;
- Creation of a structural and infrastructural environment suitable for hosting development projects.

To ensure consistency in the State-Private Sector relations in this context, ties of solidarity and a climate of trust had to be consolidated by:

- The provision of more financial resources to the National Investment Company;
- The creation of industrial domains to promote the incubation of companies with national managers;
- The search by public authorities or in association with private companies, for new export markets.

Public finance management which improved from a five-year term to another enabled an increase in budgetary savings, which rose at a 7% rate per year, i.e. CFAF 105 billion in volume over the programme forecasts according to projections.

Also, the self-financing of public companies has improved in this five-year interval; this testified to the renewed robustness of the economy, better equipped to manage the second oil shock of 1979, following the outbreak of the Iran-Iraq war. This time, the price per barrel will start at $10, and reach $20, $30, and then $40. It will never fall below these historical levels again.

Exhaustion of Support for SMEs

Following a joint evaluation in 1983, it was recognized that FOGAPE

- did not meet the set objectives,
- did not have good solutions to the difficulties of SMEs,
- did not have sufficient human, material and financial resources for its missions,
- Was weakly linked to the private sector.

This mechanism was therefore reorganized in 1984. However, even the refreshed FOGAPE did not survive the managerial flaws that have been criticized. Moreover, the lack of vision and leadership, the poor control of its provincial implementation and ineffective institutional coordination would have put an end to its existence. Governance practices dominated by corruption, clientelism, favouritism, insider trading, influence peddling and collusion will precipitate the disappearance of this precious instrument.

Ultimately, the government decided its dissolution and its replacement with a hypothetical CIC (Crédit Industriel et Commercial), which took about 30 years to actually start up. This is a pathetic case of non-creative destruction.

This period was also the period of the creation of large industrial units.

Table 10: Business creation from 1975 to 1980; capital in million CFAF

N°	COMPANY	Share capital	Field of activity	Number of employees
1	SODERIM	1,535	Cereals	400
2	CCFI	2,200	Food	120
3	MILKY WAY	600	Milk	102
4	NOBRA	5,000	Brewery	507
5	SOCAPROD	600	Drinks	256
6	SAFTL	200	Textile	30
7	SOLICAM	930	Textile	265
8	CELLUCAM	15,000	Pulp	950
9	ECAM PLAQUAGE	406	Wood	150
10	SAT PLASTIQUE	230	Plastic	71
11	SONARA	4,000	Chemical, petroleum	335
12	MICHLER METALU	150	Mechanics	100
13	GITRAM	30	Mechanics	50
14	FAEM	30	Household appliances	202
TOTAL		29,131		8,277
AVERAGE		2,080.78		591.21

Source: SYNDUSTRICAM's industrial file

CONCLUSION OF FYP-4

It is one thing to have the capital and ambitions to create and manage companies; but success depends on the ability to manage and adapt to erratic economic fluctuations. It appears that Cameroonian managers were not sufficiently equipped (if they now are) to face and then overcome the risk associated with investment and macroeconomic uncertainty. Some of them would have relied on complicity with tax and customs authorities to do business; but fraud has never been a lasting and loyal accomplice on which to build a business plan and ensure its implementation.

5. THE FIFTH FIVE-YEAR PROGRAMME FOR ECONOMIC, SOCIAL AND CULTURAL DEVELOPMENT. (FYP-5) 1981 - 1986

Results of the four previous programmes indicated that the objectives of the import substitution policy were not achieved. Even the combination with export promotion would not make much difference. Also, the chronically low energy supply and the unpredictable evolution of the global economy made it impossible to achieve industrial objectives.

The Fifth Five-Year Plan kicked off while Cameroon had been producing and exporting oil for three financial years, and the world was enduring the second oil shock. A new two-pronged strategy was adopted to equip the industrial fabric with bumpers, but also -a song already heard before- to enhance the value of local resources; this strategy focused on:

- Establishing an autonomous, self-sustaining, integrated industry, controlled by nationals and not very sensitive to external cyclical fluctuations;
- Locally enhancing the value of main natural resources.

Notwithstanding its great diversity, Cameroon industry was handicapped by many internal and external problems, including a slow evolution of value added, the constant increase in growth of that of the brewing and manufacturing industries, which were unable to revamp the growth of the national economy.

Table 1: Evolution of value added in the secondary sector from 1980/81 to 1983/84 (in billions of current CFA francs)

SECTOR	1980/81	1981/82	1982/83	1983/84
Extractive industries	201.5	263.1	400. 5	520.5
Manufacturing industries	173.7	247.0	290.9	358.5
Electricity, gas and water	17.5	22.2	30.1	35.2
Construction and Civil Engineering	103.3	125.0	145.8	192.6
Secondary GDP	496.0	657.3	867.3	1,106.8
Total GDP	**1,796.5**	**2172.8**	**2618.0**	**3105.0**
Share of Secondary GDP / Total GDP	**27.6%**	**30.3%**	**33.1%**	**34.6%**

Source: DSCN; (see FYP-6, page 133, review of FYP-5)

On the basis of these relatively modest performances, an industrial empowerment policy had been put in place. It was inspired by the theory of Endogenous Growth of Levine and Romer (1986), Barro and Lucas (1988), based on locally trained human and financial capital.

This FYP-5 was marked by a new fact: following the continuous improvement of per capita income, **Cameroon was reclassified at the end of 1983, from a Low Income Country to a Middle Income Country.** As a result, the State became eligible for international financial markets. However, authorities became afraid of increasing the debt burden and were directing development cooperation towards Islamic countries and bodies likely to provide them with soft or concessional loans. These tensions obviously did not pay off insofar as it was at that time that bold loans had to be contacted to invest in energy production, the construction of economic infrastructure and the opening up of mining or agricultural basins. Thus, private market debt policy will remain as in the past, driven by caution and precautionary forecasts of discount rates.

Financially, the public sector contributed 60% of the CFAF 1,380 billion (twice the FYP-4) projected. The rationale behind doubling the appropriations from one plan to another was once again respected: 380 billion (27%) came from outside, compared to 52% in FYP-4. Dependency on the outside thus halved because endogenous development was becoming a reality in financial programming. Private sector financing cost 13%.

Table 12: Counterparts of the monetary system (in billion CFAF)

YEARS DESIGNATION	1981/82	1982/83	1983/84
Direct public debt	96.70	191.40	165.30
Public debt servicing	26.00	30.00	46.00
Exports of goods and services	434.80	547.50	646.50
Gross Domestic Product	2,172/80	2,618/00	3,191/00
Direct debt-export ratio (%)	5.97	5.47	7.11
Direct debt- GDP ratio (%)	1.20	1.10	1.40

Source: MINFI/MINPAT; FYP-6, page 28.

These two tables show that **the fifth FYP ended in euphoria**, with all macroeconomic indicators largely green:

- The overall monetary resources have more than doubled in five years;
- Foreign assets peaked at a historic high in 1985 at 139.3 billion;

- Net claims on the State were contracting very sharply, with an unprecedented level of repayment of domestic and foreign public debt;
- Loans to the economy increased at a sustained rate, with 91% in 1984/85 compared to 1980/81;
- Exports of goods and services were doing well overall with a good contribution from raw materials: 20 to 21% of GDP between 1981/82 and 1983/84;
- The ratio of direct public debt to GDP remained low and debt service largely sustainable in relation to export revenues (7.1% of GDP in 1983/84), compared to 5.4% in 1982/83.

Such a euphoric context and good prospects for profit rates could only attract significant domestic and foreign private investment.

Table 13: Business and job creation from 1980 to 1985

	COMPANY	Share capital	Field of activity	NUMBER OF EMPLOYEES
1	International Brewery	2,400	Brewery	700
2	SITABAC	1,200	TOBACCO	302
3	SOCARTO	400	PAPER	100
TOTAL		**4,060**		**1,102**
AVERAGE		**1,152. 33**		**367**

Source: SYNDUSTRICAM's industrial file

These industrial units, which are mainly privately owned, have, despite their polluting nature, raised great hopes in terms of job opportunities. However, this hope was short-lived and turned into disillusionment.

In the end, there were no success stories. On the other hand, the anger of shareholders who felt swindled, the despair of the employees, customers and suppliers who bet heavily on these **atypical "Business Angels"**, damaged the expectations raised.

CONCLUSION OF FYP-5

The country's financial situation at the end of the FYP-5 was healthy and even very comfortable. Cameroon matched its reclassification as a middle-income country. Paradoxically, the FYP-6, which began in July 1986, was that of all disillusions. Only nine months were enough for the precious document of the Programme to be filled in the annals of history to be henceforth only consulted by researchers and curious nostalgic.

That is how the country began its abrupt descent to **the Heavily Indebted Poor Countries (HIPC);** it will take more than two decades to begin a slow and timid recovery.

6. THE SIXTH FIVE-YEAR PLAN (FYP-6) OR THE CAMEROON RENEWAL PROGRAMME: 1986 - 1991

The Stark Contrast

On the occasion of the presentation of the Sixth Five-Year Plan to Parliamentarians at the National Assembly in July 1986, President Paul BIYA gave his first development planning guidelines since his accession to supreme authority. He then stated emphatically: "**Cameroon resolutely continues its irreversible march towards the landmark encounter with the great destiny that awaits it**".

This vision was shared by all economists, analysts or forecasters, and no one could predict what would happen nine months later in a country whose external credibility and solvency were firmly established, and a GDP growing at an annual rate of 6.7%.

Four types of funding will be sought:

- Subsidies ;
- State-to-State credit (currently sovereign funds);
- Buyer credit, and
- Financial credit.

At that time, it was clearly recognized that Cameroon could only exceptionally resort to the financial market for its investments. This choice was based on the comfort provided by the mattress of export earnings from raw materials and the strength of foreign exchange reserves. But this was without taking into account the erratic evolutions of the exchange rates and more particularly of the American dollar. Rational expectations were thus thwarted by the volatility of commodity prices and the collapse of the dollar resulting from the **ultra-liberalism of President Ronald Reagan in the United States and British Prime Minister Margaret Thatcher**. This was the beginning of a global economic crisis whose consequences will affect the world economy. Its economic, social and human cost will be unprecedented in terms of the depth and sustainability of the effects on Cameroon.

Without preparing for it, the public economic authorities, advised by the IMF and the World Bank, considered a three-pronged financial strategy:

- Stabilize public finances;
- Redefine the national debt policy, and
- Define the best conditions for external borrowing.

For the first time, fiscal measures different from those already known were being put in place. The need now was to:

- register counterpart funds before the entry into force of external loan agreements;
- balance the budget from internally generated resources;
- Safeguard external solvency in the short term through a debt service ratio that evolves within reasonable limits (without specifying which ones!).

Despite these precautions, the debt burden on public revenues had apparently doubled in less than ten years, from 7.3% (1982/83) to 14% (1990/91). On the other hand, net savings had an average annual growth rate of 6.3%. These savings could have strengthened investment resources which, although having increased at an average rate of 7.3%, remained low in volume relatively to needs.

In real terms, there were almost no new projects registered under the FYP-6, and a short-term budgetary approach had been set up.

Table 14: Public finance trend (in billion CFAF permanent features of 1983)

	1982/83		1986/87		1990/91	
	Amount	%	Amount	%	Amount	%
Taxes and duties + Oil royalty	203.2	49.6	279.5	52.0	332.6	54.0
Customs duties and indirect taxes	143.7	35.0	177.3	33.0	184.8	30.0
Registration, stamp & guardianship	19.0	4.6	21.9	4.1	33.9	5.5
Other revenues	44.1	10.8	58.7	10.9	64.7	10.3
Total Revenue = Total Expenditure	410.0	100.0	537.4	100.0	616.0	100.0
Operating expenses	256.7	62.6	338.6	62.6	351.1	57.0
Debt servicing	30.0	7.3	59.1	11.0	86.3	14.0
Equipment expenditure	123.3	30.1	139.7	26.4	178.6	29.0

Source: MINPAT/MINFI; page 317 of the FYP-6 and author's projections.

Overview of Industry Indicators on the Eve of the Crisis

As at 30 June 1985, the State shareholder had more than 171 organizations in the portfolio of the National Investment Corporation of Cameroon (SNI). They accounted for 689 billion cumulative investments and 900 billion in turnover, representing 28.17% of the GDP for 1983-1984. Industrial value added stood at CFAF 174 billion with 43,758 jobs of all categories, that is 17% of the industrial workforce. The wage cost of public companies was CFAF 17.4 billion (45% of the wage bill in the manufacturing and extractive industries).

The social capital of the industrial sector: 310 billion CFA francs, divided into public shares: 63.5% (CFAF 196.85 billion) and 36.5% (CFAF 103.15 billion) for the private sector. The taxes paid amounted to CFAF 40 billion, or about 8% of the 1983/84 State Budget (which was CFAF 520 billion)[5].

New Support Measures for SMEs

- adjust and strengthen the response capacities of public agencies;
- promote a better division of labour and institutional coordination;
- involve the private sector through consultation mechanisms;
- Expand regulatory measures to support businesses.

The development potential of SMEs lies at the heart of a regional development policy that includes major equipment or development projects, rural development and environmental sustainability. The development of local raw materials had to continue to lead to a global plan for the processing of agricultural products i.e. cocoa, coffee, palm oil, peanuts, wood and derived products.

The emphasis was then placed on the development of building material industries through the valorisation of wood, pozzolan and clay as well as on electromechanical industries for domestic use, communication infrastructures, and the development of telephony.

In short, nothing really surprising except a reminder of the wishes expressed and included in the catalogue of

---

[5] Diagnostic review of FYP-5 and SNI: First reflection on retrocession.

measures to be taken throughout the country's industrial history.

Consequently, the Industrial Strategy of the FYP-6 did not bring anything new, apart from the sluggish protection of import substitution and a weak promotion of exports. It encouraged, though without success,

- the development of standardization, and
- The exploitation of patents and licenses.

These intangible assets would not add anything to operational capabilities or to the improvement of industrial efficiency.

Cameroon therefore did not have the pleasure of implementing its sixth Development Plan due to the unexpected onset of a global economic crisis.

CONCLUSION OF FYP-6

Cameroon's industrialization at FYP-6 was in stark contrast to its potential. Before the economic crisis, public administration and public sector companies provided jobs and income unrelated to competitiveness, productivity and accounting results.

Social classes began to emerge, especially the middle class made up of business executives, senior civil servants, government suppliers and large producers of agricultural cash crops. A certain local bourgeoisie was already forming, and the proletariat was not too visible because it benefited from the "trickledown effect" secreted by the oil manna and the remunerative prices of basic products.

However, from 1987 and thereafter, everything was to be redone. The emerging middle class was disintegrating and slow to reconstitute. Cameroon society, dual, was hence made up of **“the poor and the non-poor”.** National accountants, out of modesty or realism, could no longer establish objective criteria for wealth because of the instability of fortunes.

And, more than ever, all eyes were focused on the State from which everything was expecting: training, employment and income; this was the end of the welfare State.

CONCLUSION OF THE SIX FIVE-YEAR PROGRAMMES

The twenty-five years of planned and directed economy (1961 to 1986), placed Cameroonians in a kind of determinism, fatality, in the face of a future that is apparently smooth and largely predictable with regard to attainment of projections. For these reasons, planners were unable to manage the macroeconomic risk and uncertainty that occurred at the beginning of the FYP-6.

The import-substitution industrialization model was leaned on pillars which, individually or collectively, produced only meagre results compared to expectations. It would have failed to:

- replace imports with domestic production;
- reduce external dependency;
- sustainably increase the growth rate;
- Stabilize the trade balance.

The failure of this approach came from the fact that domestic production had come up against the narrowness of the domestic market, with the opportunities offered by neighbouring countries lacking in depth to the extent where their industrial structures are only identical to those in Cameroon. Other difficulties were inherent in the mobilization of funds, import of equipment and inputs, and quality of foreign technical assistance in industry.

The economic crisis that surprised forecasters in 1987 permanently placed Cameroon in the hazardous search for a relevant economic model. However, neither business models, nor the structural adjustment programme, nor debt cancellation and even less poverty reduction strategies, have brought the desired effectiveness towards the scale of the cumulative imbalances.

In the impossibility of correcting the mistakes of the past and their consequences, the urgency would have been to think and act differently; but how? What were the chances of success? Which ideological engine to adapt?

CHAPTER II:

THE VISION OF CAMEROON'S EMERGENCE BY 2035

In February 2009, the Government of Cameroon (GOC) adopted an ambitious agenda for economic development and poverty reduction known as "Vision 2035." The strategy's overarching goal was to transform Cameroon into an industrialized, upper-middle-income country with low poverty rates, strong economic growth, and a functioning democracy. To achieve its vision, the government adopted the Growth and Employment Strategy Paper (*Document de Stratégie pour la Croissance et l'Emploi*, DSCE) for 2010–2020, which targeted several objectives, including: (i) increasing the annual GDP growth rate to 5.5 percent; (ii) reducing the underemployment rate from 75.8 percent to less than 50 percent by creating tens of thousands of formal jobs each year; and (iii) lowering the monetary poverty rate from 39.9 percent in 2007 to no more than 28.7 percent.

Nine years later, a protracted slump in global oil prices has prompted Cameroon and other CEMAC member States to refocus their efforts on macro-fiscal stabilization[6]. While Cameroon's relatively diversified economy proved more resilient than those of more oil-dependent CEMAC countries, domestic challenges worsened Cameroon's economic situation. Outbreaks of

[6] The World Bank (2018), Cameroon, Public Expenditure Review. Aligning Public Expenditure with the Goal of Vision 2035.

violence in the North and Far North Regions, coupled with a secessionist movement in the country's English-speaking areas, suppressed economic activity and spurred a sharp rise in security spending. The annual GDP growth rate slowed to 3.2 percent in 2017, the lowest rate in seven years, and the fiscal deficit peaked at 6.1 percent in 2016. Meanwhile, a significant increase in borrowing to fund large infrastructure projects pushed the debt-to-GDP ratio from 15.9 percent of GDP in 2006 to 35.7 percent of GDP in 2017. Several key socioeconomic indicators have diverged from their Vision 2035 targets, including child and maternal health outcomes, and both monetary and nonmonetary measures of household wellbeing. Consequently, the intermediate objectives of the DSCE may not be achieved.

The World Bank reports that **Cameroon's total revenue has fallen between 2006 and 2014, as oil revenue gradually declined overtime, and non-oil revenue did not grow sufficiently to offset the loss in oil revenue.** Oil production and export volumes dropped significantly because of Cameroon's shrinking reserves, aging equipment, and the postponement of key investments in oil field infrastructure. Oil revenue consequently dropped from 6.1 percent of GDP in 2006 to 3.9 percent of GDP in 2014. At the same time, non-oil revenue only grew by 1 percentage point of GDP during the same period, so that overall revenue (excluding grants) fell by 1 percentage point of GDP

The Vision of Cameroon's emergence by 2035[7] is neither a self-realized dream nor an exclusively Cameroonian approach. It is part of a certain fashion trend. As ECCAS had set this horizon in 2025, it is even paradoxical that Cameroon, the supposed economic engine of the Sub-

---

[7] GESP, p.14

region, should take longer to achieve an objective for which it is at the centre of the formulation.

Fashion effect? The emergence has become a slogan, as SAP once was: “there are people who would never have been in love if they had never heard of love[8]”.

At the industrial level, The Vision 2035 announces: “Cameroon's ambition to move its economy from primary to second import substitution, with manufacturing production contributing 25% of GDP, compared to 11% currently (2010) and a secondary sector as a whole (including extractive industries) accounting for more than 40% of GDP”. To do this, it "retains the need for an industrial technological leap with an emphasis on the development of local raw materials, a change in the structure of the economy from a dominance of primary (agriculture and extraction) and informal tertiary activities, to a stage where the secondary sector will be predominant, the primary sector intensive and the professional, a tertiary sector specialized that creates decent jobs[9]”.

Thus, at the emergence, which is the final stage of this Vision, the Cameroonian’s economy will be integrated into the world’s economy both from a commercial point of view (exports and imports), as well as a financial one (opening local financial markets to external capital). In terms of pace and method, the Vision opts for accelerated investment as a driver of growth, industrial development and an ambitious trade policy. The industrialization strategy designed to reach the stage of a New Industrial Country is based on three main axes:

Is it strategic renovation or a big step backwards? Probably both, since it is a question of relying on:

---

[8] La Rochefoucauld (1613-1680) ; Maximes.

[9] GESP.

- The agricultural revolution;
- The development of extractive industries;
- The competitiveness of sectors with high growth and employment potential;
- Improving the business climate;
- The development of research, innovation and standardization.

These actions have already been planned in the recent or distant past, but without success. This time, it is probably a question of following in the footsteps of the New Industrial Countries; is this possible when the mistakes of the past are neither acknowledged nor corrected? Moreover, how can Cameroon embark on a path of catching up without drawing on local cultural resources that differ so widely from those of the reference countries?

Table 15: The main macroeconomic data (in %) for the first phase of Vision 2035

TITLE	2010	2011	2012	2013 - 2015	2016 - 2020
Real GDP	3.1	4.8	5.3	6.1	5.9
Non-oil GDP	3.8	4.5	5.1	6.2	6.2
Real GDP per capita	0.2	1.9	2.4	3.1	2.9
Non-oil revenues/GDP	12.6	12.5	12.5	12.4	12.8
Investment rate	18.6	19	19.3	19.7	22
Public investment rate	2.4	2.4	2.4	2.4	2.2
Taxes revenues/GDP	11.2	11.1	11.2	11.3	11.8
Taxes on international trade	1.7	1.7	1.6	1.3	0.8
Total government revenues	15.5	16. 5	17.2	16.8	15.8

Source: GESP, 2009.

The monotonous evolution of the GDP and other aggregates suggested that growth was staggering, slowing down from 2014 onwards, in contrast to the rate predictions that would approach or reach the two-digit level if the objectives set are to be achieved. The challenge is in total non-oil government revenues, which have been declining since 2012, and in the drivers of their resilience.

1. REALISM AS A PARADIGM IN THE INDUSTRIAL PROCESS

Realism soon contrasted with some of the romanticism that could be noticed in the unrealistic expectations of the planning expert of the time. The tendency was therefore to stay closer to reality instead of formulating a vision and managing all the opportunities and constraints associated with it. The choice of objectives and means of industrialization was from then on guided by:

- availability of local resources;
- size and evolution of markets;
- technical threshold of the production units; and
- The economic interest of industrial projects.

Apparently, there was no major change from the previous approach; but the peculiarity was based on three modalities:

1- The State identified investments and formulated hypotheses for their implementation by the private sector,

2- The private sector had full freedom to undertake and relied on incentives negotiated with the public authorities;

3- The State assessed the overall and sectorial impact of the operations carried out and reprogrammed those that had not been carried out.

The economic and social criteria taken into consideration in the evaluation process were:

- the added value;
- job creation and the wage bill distributed;
- return on invested capital;
- impact on tax revenues;
- Impact on foreign trade.

The multiplier and induced effects of investments were also analysed. Thus, in each sector, a distinction was made between projects with high profitability potential and those requiring multifaceted support from the public authorities because of their low or distant profitability.

Also, the omnipresent State began to extend its tentacles into the productive sphere. Targets were designed to enable the competent administrations to:

- improve the reception and information of investors;
- facilitate the coming in of new investors through a regional development policy;
- Stimulate reinvestment through tax and non-tax measures.

It is also during FYP-2 that the **"administered model"** of industrial governance really took shape.

In this neo-utilitarian State (Evans 1982, 1995), the central administration discovered its mission of seeking stocks and started giving out opportunities to interest groups and civil servants, who enriched themselves at the expense of social welfare. However, according to Evans, the unpredictability of the State limited investments productivity and the development of a genuine bourgeoisie.

This perception contrasts with the institutionalised conception of the State according to the approaches of

Weber, Gerschenkron and Hirschman, who propose the existence of complementarities between State structures and the market in the industrialization process. This is the connivance capitalism that refers to the Developmental State; characteristic of Asian countries. By transforming into a welfare state, Cameroon seemed to be abusing realism by becoming "Pro[10] " several times: **Prospector-Programmer- Producer - Promoter - Protector - Professional - Provoker - Pro-polluter**. The list of epithets could be extended, but those listed show that authoritarian planning took precedence over liberalism. Since administration and bureaucracy had inhibited entrepreneurial freedom to undertake the accumulation process reduced due to the invasion of regulation and repressive control of market prices. However, while the Octopus State sought to extend its influence over activity sectors, an interactive governance model based on sociological or cultural proximity was being built and structured at the micro, meso and social levels. It was supported by the private sector, liberal professions and extended to the informal sector. This is the so-called **"reticular model"**.

2. THE MANAGEMENT OF THE ECONOMIC CRISIS AND THE PARADIGM SHIFT

The crisis, which erupted due to the combined effect of the collapse of oil prices, the depreciation of the US dollar and the sudden erosion of agricultural commodity prices (cocoa, coffee, bananas, wood, tobacco), caused a 50% drop in export revenues, which fell from CFAF 1102 billion

[10] Jean-Raphaël CHAPONNIERE (Research Engineer at the Institute of Economic Research, Production and Development (IREPD) URA CNRS and Pierre JUDET (Professor at the University Pierre-Mendes-France (Grenoble) Researcher at the IREPD: " (Asian Industrial Dynamics: Lessons for Africa) "

in 1985/86 to CFAF 550 billion in 1986/87. The deterioration in economic activity had a negative impact on the Treasury's revenue, which fell by 40% between 1985 and 1987, while the pressure of debt service payment deadlines scared the managers of the State coffers. The budget deficit for 1986/87 alone was CFAF 508 billion, a figure reduced to CFAF 214 billion in 1987/88 thanks to the austerity measures introduced in the Finance Act.

The ratio of outstanding public debt to GDP increased from 19% in 1984/85 to 98.8% in 1994/95. At the same time, the debt-to-export ratio jumped from 11% to 43%, while payment arrears accumulated both domestically and externally.

Beyond the deterioration in the terms of trade of about 32% between 1986/87 and 1991/92, the crisis also revealed the ineffectiveness of the growth policies and strategies implemented since 1960. These weaknesses can be summarized as follows:

1°) an international trade structure dominated by the export of primary products with low added value;

2°) a manufacturing industry oriented towards the domestic market sheltered from foreign competition by an arsenal of protectionist measures that created monopoly situations without developing real resilience capacities;

3°) The very high price of the CFA franc, which contributed to the increase in Cameroon exports.

The combination of these distortions would have produced two devastating effects, including:

(i) the encouragement to consume imported products through an overvalued currency;
(ii) The development of an import substitution industry that was capital intensive and focused on domestic

markets, whose solvency had deteriorated significantly.

This new context benefited the Bretton Woods institutions Consultants and imposed the **Structural Adjustment Programme (SAP)** as a miracle cure and the only way out of the crisis. The sick Cameroon resigned itself to this generic treatment, since other developing countries stuck in similar difficulties were prescribed same.

While keeping its sixth five-year plan in its drawers, the Government committed to finding alternative solutions in industrial matters. Thus, with the technical and financial support of UNDP and UNIDO, an Industrialization Master Plan (IMP) was urgently prepared and adopted in 1988, which was considered a **"compass for the methodical and rational management of the country's industrialization[11]"**; according to Paul BIYA, in the foreword to the IMP. This Plan was largely based on the social project formulated in his masterpiece entitled **"For the Community Liberalism".**

This IMP was not lacking in audacity, on the contrary. However, a Plan is not a Policy. The Plan makes it possible to set for a medium-term horizon, the evolution of economic aggregates and the qualitative changes associated with this evolution; while an economic policy integrates the different macroeconomic model variables on which the decision-maker can intervene in the short, medium and long term, to set objectives and priorities in terms of growth, employment, inflation and external equilibrium.

What Cameroon's President was really thinking was that, the solution would lie in the freedom to undertake, the

---

[11] The Ministry of Programming and Regional Development, Ministry of Trade and Industry (1988), The Cameroon Industrialization Master Plan; Cameroon News and Publishing Corporation, Yaoundé.

regulatory function of a democratic State and the duty of solidarity. In the IMP, industry's competitiveness is one of the essential components of the modernization of the economy of Cameroon, just behind agriculture, which is considered top priority.

Due to its purely technical nature, the IMP would not have succeeded in inventing a new trajectory. Some of the levers it had targeted again were drawn from the past:

1) Support for SMEs and SMIs;
2) Priority to the agro-food, animal and fishing industries;
3) progressive development of heavy industry;
4) geographical balance of industrial locations;
5) fair distribution of income generated by industrial activity;
6) ecologically rationalized management;
7) Mastery of science, technology and research-development.

More specifically, the IMP would have set guidelines for the short- and medium-term modernization of activities in the sectors of building materials, metallurgy, steel, forestry and hydrocarbon resources development.

This figure skating has not escaped criticism from some experts, including Boniface MBALLA MBALLA, a Cameroonian economist: "The IMP was limited to guidelines, whereas it should have indicated the objectives pursued and the source of the means to ensure its financing[12]". In any case, the logic behind this IMP made the agro-food industries the first choice of Cameroon's

---

[12] Mbala Mbala, Boniface (2010), in an article of the newspaper "*Mutations*", dated 16/02/2010, entitled ''Failure on the springs of industrialization)''. An investigation by Pierre Celestin Atangana.

industrialization process. This choice, which was anything but a revolution, was justified by the existence of **natural advantages**, while neoliberal economic theory required the creation of **new comparative advantages.**

Another paradigmatic shift occurred at the end of the 1990s, with the transition from the Structural Adjustment Programme (SAP) to the **Poverty Reduction Strategy (PRS).**

3. INDUSTRIAL COMPETITIVENESS AND THE PRSP[13]

The 1990s was marked by a sharp contraction in the incomes of economic players (government, companies, and households) and loss of industrial competitiveness in terms of cost and non-cost. Even the effect of the devaluation of the CFA franc in January 1994, which gave a slight boost to exports of agricultural and mining products, was not enough to create a sufficient exciting impulse to strengthen exportable industrial production. To be realistic, the government attempted to resize its ambitions by revaluing them to the manufacturing industry as if these were a strategic innovation; under the pretext of the promotion of general competitiveness and support for the development of agro-food, textile and wood processing sectors to increase the industry's contribution to growth.

These options were prompted by studies on "**Sources of Growth and Competitiveness**", conducted according to a supply chain approach and oriented towards "**the development of textile/confection clusters, poultry industries, tertiary wood processing**" (Cf. PRSP Executive Summary, page xii). Besides, investment in the agro-food industry was classified in an uncertain

[13] Growth and Employment Strategy Paper (GESP), August 2009; Government/MINEPAT.

perspective because raw materials that supplied the industry were also food for a rapidly growing population. The available food was also awaited by households in neighbouring countries (Nigeria, Chad, Gabon, Guinea and Central African Republic).

According to Bernard Gauthier, "SAP introduced profound changes in the industrialization strategy and the political and economic environment of companies[14]". A survey he carried out makes it possible to identify the main constraints to the success of the recommended adjustment measures.

Table 16: Main constraints to competitiveness (in % of respondents)

CONSTRAINTS	SIZE OF THE COMPANY					SECTOR	
	Total	Micro	Small	Medium	Large	Informal	Formal
Lack of appropriations	52	57	63	42	29	65	47
-Insufficient request	43	51	41	47	37	43	41
-Imports competition		16	14	12	6	7	19
-Exports competition	16	0	7	7	6	0	8
Lack of infrastructure	14	14	15	7	23	17	13
-Price of services	6	3	8	0	11	4	7
- Taxes	24	14	19	42	26	20	25
-Corruption	20	0	23	28	26	4	26
-Industrial strategy	1	5	12	20	26	7	17
-Subsidies		11	11	16	3	9	11
-Assistance to companies		8	9	7	0	11	6

Source: Bernard Gauthier, 1996

[14] Gauthier B. (1996): "*Dynamics of the African Manufacturing Sector in a Period of Structural Adjustment. A Case Study of Cameroon*".In Revue Région et Développement n°3-1996., Institute of Applied Economics, Ecole des Hautes Etudes Commerciales, Montreal, Canada.

Table 17: Average annual growth rates 1961- 1993

	1961/66	1967/71	1972/78	1979/86	1987/93
Growth rate (%) actual GDP	4.1	+1.0	6.4	+9.1	-5.0
Agriculture	-2.4	+4.6	+3.2	+5.2	-4.7
Industry	+16.0	+6.0	+6.4	+18.0	-6.1
Manufacturing	+17.3	+6.1	+2.7	+14.2	-7.7
Services	+6.7	-2.8	+6.6	+7.7	-4.4
In GDP %					
Agriculture	39.5	36.6	34.5	25.6	22.5
Industry	15.4	16.7	16.8	31.9	30.1
Manufacturing	0.5	10.5	10.1	10.6	12.9
Services	45.1	46.8	48.6	42.0	47.4

Sources: B. Gauthier, J. P LeGoff and L. Vallée[15] *(under the supervision of B. Gauthier) 1995.*

Despite the upheavals caused by so many constraints, the need to seek another alternative was self-evident.

4. ECONOMY INDUSTRIAL COMPETITIVENESS AND CONSTRAINTS

Since 2004, the political discourse has placed competitiveness, productivity and creativity at the heart of its industrial strategy. To achieve this, the following were required

- A major industrial policy, and
- Development of the energy capacity.

The challenge then resided in building a tunnel to a promised land, casting out arrogance, ideological intimidation, the superiority complex of influence networks, and establishing platforms where people would respect each other and listen to advocacies for efficiency and excellence. This seemingly romantic challenge in the on-going state of mind-sets would be overcome by strategic

---

[15] Under the supervision of Bernard Gauthier (1995): Crisis of the State and the Manufacturing Sector in Cameroon, World Bank, Annex I, Table 19.

inclusion of all political, administrative, corporate, intellectual and associative categories of the country.

Competitiveness of the Agricultural Sectors: A Poorly Controlled Operating Mode

From one generation of economic policy makers to another, by wisdom or stubbornness, the use of the supply chain approach happened to be the essential path to Cameroon's industrialization. Although this option had not produced satisfactory results for fifty years, it was still subject to a surprising doctrinal renewal.
A major step backwards had thus been taken in the field of industrial strategy. To be in line with theory, sector competitiveness sought to promote the development of an integrated set of companies located at different stages of the production process for the same set of products. This networking consisted in favouring interdependent and complementary activities within a group of companies in order to benefit from the synergy effect.

Choosing this strategy implied pursuing a global policy aimed at strengthening the coherence and gradual interlinking of business segments. As success of a sector strategy depends on the importance of the upstream segments, R & D up to the downstream after-sales service of finished products. More concretely, the architecture of a supply chain is only complete if it makes all the upstream, intermediate and downstream joints of a product work. Given that actors of each node are interdependent, the rupture of a segment would be enough to handicap the sector.

Designing a supply chain consists in detailing all the elementary operations that make it possible to transform a raw material into a finished product intended for final consumption. This configuration led the strategist to take into consideration transformation stages that brought more value and the control of coordination between different links in search of specific agreements with stakeholders.

The revamping of the sector policy to the product policy in Cameroon did not allow the construction of dynamics sufficient for the emergence of an industrialization process. The surprise was the discourse on the sectors which had become increasingly focused on agriculture mainly on so-called cash crops: cocoa, coffee, rubber, cotton, palm oil, wood, whose transformation rates remained desperately insignificant.

The entrenchment of industrial development in the sector could have given a false sense of security to the economy and led to an underestimation of the difficulties of vertical integration. The major weakness of agro-industrialization by the sector was also found in the discontinuities in productivity gains at the level of the different links; hence the need to consider the complexity of the economic system and the problem of transmission of effects between products and between different sectors.

Since the purpose of economic activity was not the development of a product, but rather growth, sharing of results and impacts, emphasis was to be placed on the managerial efficiency of institutions and the attractiveness of the business environment. So, from the moment that the sector focused on product development, it no longer had its doctrinal relevance.

More specifically, agricultural sectors in Cameroon were inconsistent.

Each segment operated independently; meanwhile the combination of activities should have been the rule for value sharing, risk and efficiency gains. As a result, "companies were locked into an insular and inward looking reflection, which was seen in the reluctance of companies to bring their customers, suppliers and business partners together within a large corporate machine[16]". Cocoa, coffee, cotton, rubber, wood and palm oil production, which should have been powerful agro-industrial levers, still showed processing rates of less than 5% in an economy that systematically imported chemical and technological inputs. This inevitably perpetuated the international division of labour and chronic specialization in the export of low-value raw materials.

Competitiveness based on the sector therefore presented shortcomings because it did not allow for competition analysis in all its productive, technological, financial, commercial, cultural and geostrategic composition.

Table 18: Agricultural sectors based on ecological advantages

PRIORITY SUB-SECTORS	YIELDS (TONS/HA)			PRODUCTION OBJECTIVES (TONS)		
	2010	2015	2020	2010	2015	2020
Cocoa	0.7	0.9	1.2	250,000	320,000	640,000
Arabica coffee	0.4	0.6	0.8	12,000	25,000	35,000
Robusta coffee	0.5	0.7	0.7	50,000	100,000	125,000
Cotton	1.1	1.35	1.8	120,000	150,000	200,000
Rubber	1.3	1.4	1.5	55,000	65,000	75,000
Pineapple	40	40	40	130,000	150,000	170,000
Palm oil	1.3	1.5	1.8	235,000	300,000	450,000
Maize	2.5	2.7	4.5	1,500, 000	2000, 000	4,000,000
Millet/sorghum	1.7	2	2	1,100,000	1300, 000	1,500,000
Irrigated rice	3.5	5	5	50,000	75,000	175,000
Rained rice	1.75	2.25	3	50,000	130,000	825,000
Cassava	18	20	22	3,000,000	3750, 000	4,500, 000
Yam	11	13	14	400,000	450,000	500,000
Cocoyam	10	10	10	1,500,000	1750, 000	2,000,000
Plantain	9	12	15	2,600,000	3000, 000	5,000,000
Export bananas	21	25	25	300,000	350,000	400,000

Source: Ministry of Agriculture and Rural Development

[16] An article by Sagren Moodley: "Perspectives and Challenges of e-business for the South African automotive parts sector; in, Electronic Commerce and Development", published in OECD Development Centre Studies, under the supervision of Andrea Goldstein and David O' Connor.

Potentially, natural capital, especially soil quality, still represented 30 to 50% of agricultural inputs. On the other hand, despite the enormous water resources, the irrigation rate in Cameroon agriculture stood at less than 5%, while it was 35 to 57% in Asian countries. Jacques Diouf ironically commented: "rivers in Africa are slowly flowing into the sea, as if the sea had asked them for water[17] "

In other words, insufficient agricultural competitiveness is not inevitable; it is the result of vague investment choices, poor targeting in hydro-agricultural development and land fertilization. Thus, after half a century of industrial management based on the same tools, the results were out of step with expectations; and the rehabilitation of the sector concept was somehow surprising. This reversal could be interpreted as a strategic failure to make the sector a strategic renewal and an irreplaceable path to industrialization. The cotton/textile sector reconfigured in 2008 by the government of Cameroon is an illustration of another missed opportunity for competitiveness and the achievement of industrialization objectives per sector.

The Case of Textiles

Cotton is the third most important economic activity in Cameroon. It generates 11% of the value added of the manufacturing sector and represented 9.5% of national industrial production in 2008. This sector consists of seven sub-sectors: - raw cotton- ginning - spinning - weaving - deep-drawing - hosiery - manufacturing and marketing.

In 2008, cotton production was ensured by 350,000 farmers concentrated in the three northern Regions (Adamawa, North and Far North), who sell their product

[17] By Jacques Diouf (23 April 2008), former Director General of FAO (Food and Agriculture Organization), in an interview with Radio France Internationale.

directly to SODECOTON for ginning, oil production for human consumption, and cattle meal. Spinning, stamping, manufacturing, weaving and knitting take place in a few industrial units located mainly in Douala. The industrial process remained totally dependent on an ineffective combination of factors that contributed to weakening cotton development.

Table 19: Constraints to the optimal profitability of this sector have been identified.

CATEGORY	CONTRAINTS
Sector-based policy	- Lack of strategic vision for the industry
Organizational and Institutional	- Weak synergy between different players: producers of the raw product, fabric producers, creators of industrial units; - Lack of a specific consultation framework between players of the industry and various stakeholders
Technological expertise	- Disorganized traditional production; - Lack of specialization; - Low production capacity in terms of volume, quality and lead time; -traditional working method, - Under-utilization of production capacity; - Lack of standards and quality criteria
Cost of production resources	- Low labour productivity; - Very high production cost; - Deficit in basic infrastructure (energy, road, etc.)
Governance	- Sector particularly affected by fraud, counterfeiting, smuggling and dumping of competitors - Industry controls only 1% of the national market.
Sector support system	- No specific support actions; - No promotional actions; - No appropriate funding mechanism.
Human Resources	- Insufficient training and manpower qualification; - Non-harmonized training standards and training programmes in sewing.
Other factors include	- Little developed marketing function - Low participation in promotional events at the national, regional or international level

MINEPAT, 2008.

A devaluation of the weaving warp - knitting - dyeing - tailoring - spinning - embroidery - non-woven fabrics activities and processing of ginned cotton waste into fleece reflected the sector's low contribution to GDP. Industrial solution here required the creation of clusters of textile companies for their strategic positioning in the face of global competition.

Recent introduction of the Value Chain into public discourse was an attempt to bring about changes on the value chain concept.

5. VALUE CHAIN APPROACH: THE MOST OVERLOOKED

Management by sector did not provide companies with the desired competitive advantage because of the discontinuities in the functioning of the segments; hence the need to use a process breakdown method into relevant and strategically coherent activities. The management of the productive potential induced by vertical integration proved to be better addressed through value chain, making it possible to build a matrix-type reflection on a segment, unlike the linear or simply "wired" approach required by the value chain approach.

Michael Porter finds in the value chain, "activities aimed to - design- manufacture- market- distribute- and - support the product[18]", which help in the understanding of cost behaviour and in capturing existing or potential sources of profit. It is these activities that produce value for the company; and value creates a competitive advantage for the customer, enabling the reduction of costs and improvement of performance.

---

[18] Michael Porter (1990) in "The Competitive Advantage"

A firm engaged in the competitive arena seeks to maximize the value of its core and support activities. According to M. Porter, the following are classified as core activities:

1) **internal logistics**: reception, storage, handling, warehousing, stock control, transport and customer liaison;
2) **production:** factor combination for the production of finished products through the operation of machines, assembly, packaging, equipment maintenance, printing and installation operations;
3) **external logistics**: collection, storage and distribution of products to customers, operation of delivery vehicles, order processing;
4) **marketing and sales:** advertising, promotion, sales force, selection of distribution channels, relationship with distributors and pricing;
5) **Services:** installation- repair- training- product adaptation.

The so-called support activities are based on supply systems, technological development and human resources management.

From this architecture, each firm designed its own standard chain of value-creating activities, technologies and specific economic mechanisms. The inclusive linearity developed by the value chain approach encompasses the activities of a firm's suppliers upstream and those of its customers downstream, with a view to overall efficiency.

The value chain approach does not simply focus on the segmentation and mechanical sequencing of the transformation process within the same product family, but on the mutual enrichment of activities within a company.

The Government tried to implement the competitiveness and economic growth clusters.

Competitiveness Clusters

A competitiveness cluster brings together companies, research laboratories and training institutions in a given area to develop synergies, cooperation and partnerships. This policy is based on the spill over effects of the most dynamic sectors on the economy as a whole (Hirschman, 1958). The challenge was to build on the complementarities and innovations that enable companies involved taking leading positions at the local or international level. In terms of objectives, this was about strengthening economic competitiveness, developing growth and employment, increasing innovation, strengthening activities and improving the attractiveness of the production site.

The strategies usually implemented consisted of building partnerships between different actors in the medium term, building collaborative projects that could benefit from public assistance and development partners, and promoting a global environment that was favourable to business.

Competitiveness clusters have an asset, namely economic convergence, which make it possible to coordinate reception and support systems for companies in a given territory. In a federative dynamics, they link together a pool of jobs with multidisciplinary skills, with companies that have made a name according to the site engineering, all framed in a public/private partnership. This approach was relatively part of the regional planning policy. The benefit of competitiveness clusters was the spread through business lines and activities; of strategic, technological, instrumental and operational complementarities and the sharing of added value. It helped develop economic intelligence, a major asset for companies in a context of fierce competition.

Cameroon had tried unsuccessfully to implement the competitiveness cluster approach because it had narrowed it to sector-based priorities alone, while it also required a clear and comprehensive vision, respect for the financing modalities of the choices made, and effective leadership. Thus, a competitiveness cluster could have been created in Edea in the vicinity of ALUCAM if the CELLUCAM project had been completed.

The Expertise of Competitiveness Clusters in Agro-poles

The Government re-engaged in an economic foresight by combining demographic change, the potential of natural production basins determined by ecology, financing constraints and organizational changes. The demand for the transformation of primary products in order to conquer the international market was at the core of concerns; but the main challenge remained the quantitative, qualitative and regular production of the commodities to be transformed so that shortages or stock shortages in the industry's supply could be avoided.

Agro-poles programme consists of "identifying existing production basins and developing companies for the production, processing and marketing of plant, animal, fish and forest products[19]". They host "medium-sized agricultural holdings, small producers and support infrastructures[20]". Without drawing lessons from the past, this approach is again managed like the sector policy,

---

[19] Ministry of the Economy, Planning and Regional Development (2010): Economic Program for Regional Development, for Medium and Large Enterprises in the Rural Sector in Cameroon.
[20] Ditto

whereas it is a cluster approach. More concretely, the criteria for selecting production basins are set, the operating mode defined, as well as the selection of promoters and the methods of financing projects. Speculations are also chosen namely, maize, rice, plantain banana, manioc, oil palm, cocoa, coffee, millet/sorghum, fruit and vegetables, sheep, goat, poultry, pig breeding, fish farming, fishing, wood. They are design to meet a fourfold objective:

1. Food security,
2. trade balance,
3. added value,
4. Job creation.

Issues related to processing and conservation technologies and distribution channels are not addressed at all in this scenario, nor are the energy requirement and ownership of standards to tackle international markets. To effectively implement agro-pole, measures must be put in place to increase supply and quality by combining vision, leadership, management, financing, incentives and geo-economics. Reforms should respond to the demand for control of the domestic food market, market penetration in neighbouring countries including Nigeria and ECCAS, niche by niche, and be updated as the situation evolves.

CONCLUSION

To be effective, agro-industrial competitiveness requires a strong cohesion of the different segments: R&D - innovation - seed extension - financing - production - logistics - packaging - processing - distribution - marketing. It therefore requires a close mobilization of several actors: State - researchers - producers - industrialists - traders - local authorities - non-governmental organizations - technical and financial partners.

The government's responsibility is therefore total as coordinator, regulator and instigator. Therefore, it should:

- set up an agricultural geopolitics and product specialization;
- solve the energy equation;
- build technology and transport infrastructure;
- create an agro-industrial monitoring system, diagnostic and evaluation circles;
- Engage in fruitful cooperation with ECCAS countries and Nigeria to develop mutually beneficial cross-border industrial policies; combine efficiency in value chains with a vision of competitiveness based on export incentives.

CHAPTER III:

THE CHALLENGE OF INDUSTRIAL COMPETITIVENESS FOR EMERGENCE

Cameroon's claim to become an industrialized country consisted in dragging the economy into a process of accumulating productive capital and strengthening its autonomy in manufactured products.

A Rapid Glance on the Country's routing

In the 1960s, the country exported raw or semi-processed agricultural materials, and the revenues from these exports were used to build an industrial sector that had become, against all expectations, a place of devaluating human resources and the de-accumulation of financial capital.

At the beginning of the 21st century, Cameroon's industrial landscape was still characterized by a constellation of very small and small and medium sized businesses with a production tool close to the craft industry. This proto-industry was unable to develop real links with large groups established in high-tech and intensely capital-intensive sectors. These transnational firms, which did not have a real foothold in the local productive fabric, acted as territorial enclaves for some or as mere trading posts for others.

Cameroon's production system is also configured by a proliferation of subcontracting microstructures in ICT (Information and Communication Technologies) for distribution and retail, as well as by motorcycle taxi drivers, repairers, craftsmen, handy men of all sorts. This highly disjointed system lacks coordination and perspective; consequently, duality and persistent discontinuities do not facilitate either secretion or transmission of an influx sufficient to boost the nervous system of domestic industry. The diagnosis made in the GESP (paragraphs 105 and 107) is fully in line with this assertion: the Cameroonian industry is still dominated by extractive activities, with those in manufacturing accounting for only 8% of GDP. The companies operate in an environment plagued by several factors of low competitiveness, and whose constraints are:

- Red Tape and Transaction Costs;
- Problems of internal governance, incivility and weak managerial capacities of promoters;
- The non-existence of training support and R & D infrastructures.

From its own diagnosis, the Government proposes:

- The relaunch of sector policies in a regional and global perspective;
- The current state of the industrial fabric;
- The urgent development of a coherent industrial policy by updating the IDP (Industrial Development Program) and defining priority sectors.

These three answers clearly do not include any innovation. This is a return to a policy, based on sectors with export promotion that did not flourish in the third and sixth five-year plans.

As for the current state of the industrial fabric, the 1988 IDP had done an in-depth of this; but it curiously led to the preparation of the PRSP, the fate of which is well known.

The novelty therefore seems to be "**the urgent development of a coherent industrial policy**".

Again, one wonders what happened to the 2004 presidential statement: "**Greater Achievements**" will only be possible if there is a "**real transformation of our economy**", a transformation conditioned by the formulation of a "**Major Industrial Policy**".

Once again, the languor of a techno-bureaucracy and an administrative techno-plutocracy which was allergic to competitiveness, creativity and innovation failed to respond to guidelines developed at the highest political level. Yet economic and industrial battles are won through the strength of ideas, productivity, innovation and creativity. The results of the General Business Census (GBR) of the National Statistical Institute (NSI) in 2009; analysed in 2011, provide illuminating data on the industrial landscape at the end of the first decade of the 21st century.

Table 20

Box 3: Criteria of the Ministry of SMEs, Social Economy and Handicrafts

Investments and turnover in CFA francs

Criteria	Micro enterprise (VSE)	Small Enterprise (SE)	Small and Medium-Sized (SME-SMI)	Large Enterprise (LE)
Number of employees	0 -5	5 -20	20 -50	More than 50
Initial investment	Up to 200,000	Up to 500,000	Up to one billion	More than a billion
Turnover	Up to 500,000	Up to 500,000	Up to one billion	More than a billion

National Institute of Statistics

The Trend Erosion of the Industry's Weight

Over a period of more than ten years (1993-1994 to 2004-2005), the relative weight of the industry has been steadily declining. The stagnation of industrial employment, reflected in an average annual growth rate of less than 1% since 2003, called for a strategic reorientation of investment. At the end of this period, it can be seen that manufacturing industries were insufficiently developed while agro-industry and the food industry dominated with about 50% of the branch's total production. Heavy and capital goods industries were struggling to emerge in a national market considered narrow.

1. THE SECTOR PERFORMANCE

The industrial structure is therefore spun off from small and medium-sized industries: food, clothing, construction. It is characterized by a lack of interaction between branches and sectors of activity. On the other hand, the extractive industries are preponderant, highly capital-intensive, labour-saving and mainly controlled by multinationals.

Table 21: The comparative evolution of the weight of industry in the economy (in relation to GDP)

Formulation In Relative Share	1965 – 1966	1993 – 1994	1995 – 1999	2000 – 2004	2004 – 2005	2005 – 2006	GAP 65/66-2005/2006
Primary sector	47 %	20.40%	20.24%	20.28%	20.88%	17.6%	-29.4 points
Secondary sector	14 %	36.1%	32.8%	31.1%	26.6%	34.9%	+20.9 points
Tertiary sector	39 %	27.2%	29.3%	32.7%	35.8%	47.5%	+8.5 points

Source: Authors calculations

The growing development of the service sector is reinforced by activities booming in retail trade, public transport and mobile telephony. The microfinance sub-sector has been expanding rapidly since the early 2000s. The agricultural sector still employs more than 60.6% of Cameroon's active population, but food production is generally insufficient to meet the food needs of a growing population.

This dual agricultural system (traditional agriculture for self-consumption and extroverted industrial agriculture) could not get the economy off the ground despite the many programmes jointly funded by development cooperation. Industrial agriculture employs an abundant unskilled and low-paid workforce. The still very high number of people working in the rural sector constitutes an important labour reserve that needs to be transferred from an education-training process to manufacturing and service sectors where jobs are better paid.

Overall, exogenous shocks and increased poverty were incapable of disrupting strategic choices to the extent where they could change the sector redistribution key of investment resources. This remark is corroborated by Pr. Séraphin Magloire FOUDA of the University of Yaoundé II, who notes that economic structures continue to act in an indifferent way; they are thus not very sensitive to policy changes.

Likewise, it recommends increasing conservation and processing capacities to set in motion the factors of production following the trinomial: Production-Conservation- Transformation, capable of successfully distorting the national demand curve, stimulating productivity gains with a direct effect on lower prices, higher GDP growth and labour migration to other sectors.

This industrialization model is actually nothing more than an import-substitution model whose management will once again face the constraints already mentioned. In these circumstances, the State would have to its regulatory power to restructure and implement incentives that would make new industries attractive.

The low capital intensity in the economy of Cameroon has led to a loss of industrial competitiveness compared to the countries of Sub-Saharan Africa and Emerging Asia

Table 22: Comparison of Export Performance Indicators

country	Exports of goods and services % of GDP		Export of raw materials (% of exported goods)		Export of manufacturing goods (% goods exported)		High-tech export (% of goods exported)	
	1980	2002	1980	2002	1980	2002	1980	2002
Cameroon	28	27	96	93	4	7	3	1
Ivory Coast	35	48	95	85	5	21	..	3
Ghana	8	43	99	85	1	16	..	3
Kenya	28	27	88	76	12	24	4	10
Nigeria	29	38	100	100	0	0	..	0
Senegal	27	31	85	49	15	51	..	4
Botswana	50	51	..	9	..	91	..	0
Mauritius Islands	51	61	73	27	27	73	1	2
South Africa	35	34	82	37	18	63	..	5
Malaysia	30	114	81	19	19	79	38	58
Thailand	24	65	75	22	25	74	21	31
Singapore	..	..	53	11	47	85	40	60
South Korea	33	40	10	8	90	92	18	32

Source: World Development Indicators 2004[21].

[21] According to the World Bank Indicators: manufactures comprise commodities in section 5 (chemicals), 6 (basic manufactures), 7 (machinery and transport equipment) and 8 (miscellaneous manufactured goods).

Ivory Coast beats Cameroon by several lengths in the export of manufactured and high-tech products; its lag with Malaysia speaks for itself.

Thus, the challenges Cameroon faces in terms of rebuilding its production system are immense in a context of poverty and underemployment. Opportunities are timidly exploited and production potential poorly developed due to poorly implemented investment choices.

Compared to the countries of Asia and Africa with which Cameroon had the same level of development fifty years ago, the indicators speak for themselves. The competitiveness comparators used above show the limited progress made between 1980 and 2002. There has been a significant decline in exports of technology goods, which have fallen by 66% in 22 years. Yet it is in this area that the results of industrial policies and strategies are most expected.

2. BUSINESS DEMOGRAPHICS IN 2009: NUMBER OR QUALITY?

Of the 11,685 companies counted by the NIS, 85% (9,917) were very small enterprises (VSE), compared to about 2% of LE (large enterprises). The remainder, 13%, represents SMEs.

In terms of sectorial concentration, 54.7% of these companies were created in textiles, clothing, leather and footwear. In the GE category, 25% of industrial units were in food, beverages and tobacco; 18% in wood, paper, printing and publishing, 17% in chemicals, oil refining, rubber and plastics. These three branches accounted for about 60% of light industry and still used obsolete technologies. The real issue was therefore not to celebrate the high birth rate of companies stimulated by the facilitation of procedures, but their life expectancy or their ability to be competitive, and to create value and jobs. The reforms initiated should focus on instrumental, organizational, operational and financial support for these new-borns. To this end, new decentralized technical or financial structures should provide a horizontal framework for new production units in different phases of their life cycle.

Another topic of reflection was Cameroon's position in the ranking of the top 500 African companies. A ranking published by Jeune Afrique Hors-série n°32, 2013 edition, provided sufficient information on the observed performances.

Table 23: Performance of Cameroon Large Enterprises

COMPANY	SECTORS	RANKINGS		TURNOVER 103	NET RESULTS 103
		2013	2012		
National Refining Company	Hydrocarbon	76	104	1,935,790	ND.
National Hydrocarbon Company	Hydrocarbo n	83	86	1,809, 850	43,111
Société Anonyme de Brasseries	Beverages	246	229	563,189	87,342
AES Africa Power Co.	Energy distribution	297	305	429,884	156
MTN Cameroon	Mobile network	308	500	419,667	56,191
Orange Cameroun	Mobile network	362	378	330,671	56,451
CFAO Cameroon	Diversified	405	405	290,516	ND.

Source: data reconstituted from Jeune Afrique Hors-Série n°32, 2013 edition

According to these scores, only two public companies in the Hydrocarbons sector appear in the TOP 100 (76th and 83rd rank); the Brasseries du Cameroun, a subsidiary of the French Castel Group, occupied the 246th position ahead of the two mobile telephone companies, MTN and Orange subsidiaries of global groups from South Africa and France respectively. In this continental ranking, South Africa lead the pack, followed by North Africa as a regional economic community. The first company in sub-Saharan Africa operating in the non-oil sector is Nigerian (Dangote Cement); ranked 107th in 2013, up four positions from 2012. In the agro-food sector, the SIFCA group of Côte d'Ivoire was ranked 145th. This ranking confirmed the one carried out in April 2007 by the monthly AFRICAN BUSINESS[22] in which no Cameroonian firm was ranked among the top 200 on the continent. Similarly, no Cameroonian company was found eligible in AFRICA'S TOP 250 COMPANIES in April 2013. On the other hand, there was confirmation of the domination of South African, Nigerian, Egyptian, Mauritian, Moroccan, Kenyan and Botswana companies. These rankings raise the question of the role that multinational beer and telephone companies can play in making the dream of emergence in 2035 a reality

---

[22] African Business n° 330: Africa's Top 200 Companies, African Business' annual ranking; April 2007.

Table 24: Structure (in %) of industrial enterprises by branch of activity

Type of industry	% of enterprises	VSE	SE	ME	LE
Extractive industries	0.2	0.1	0.6	0.7	3.5
Food, beverages and tobacco	5.9	3.7	14.1	21.5	24.6
Textiles, clothing, leather and shoes	54.7	63.4	10.5	1.7	1.9
Wood, paper, printing and publishing industry	9.3	7.8	13.1	22.8	17.7
Chemistry, refining, rubber, plastic	0.8	0.2	1.3	2.8	16.5
Materials for metal constructions and foundries	8.2	7.6	6.1	19.2	8.5
Metal structures electrical appliances, transport	0.9	0.6	1.8	3.9	3.1
Other manufacturing industries	13.7	13.7	29.1	1.0	1.5
Electricity, gas and water	0.6	0.2	1.1	1.8	10.8
Construction	5.7	2.8	22.3	24.6	11.9
TOTAL	100.0	100.0	100.0	100.0	100.0

Source: NIS/GEC 2009

Table 25: Structure (in %) according to the size of the company.

Type of industry	Total	VSE	SE	ME	LE
Extractive industries	100.0	24.0	20.0	20.0	36.0
Food, beverages and tobacco	100.0	52.5	16.1	22.2	9.2
Textiles, clothing, leather and shoes	100.0	98.4	1.3	0.2	0.1
Wood, paper, printing and publishing industry	100.0	71.1	9.6	15.0	4.2
Chemistry, oil refinery, rubber and plastic	100.0	20.7	10.9	21.7	46.7
Metal and foundries construction material	100.0	78.3	5.0	14.3	2.3
Metal structures electrical appliances and transport equipment	100.0	53.7	13.0	25.9	7.4
Other manufacturing industries	100.0	84.9	14.4	0.4	0.3
Electricity, gas and water	100.0	32.4	12.2	17.6	37.8
Construction	100.0	42.2	26.7	26.5	4.7
Total	100.0	84.9	6.8	6.1	2.2

Source: NIS/GEC 2009

Several public companies are considered as State Milk Cow organizations, when they are not Dilemmas or Dead Weights. Most of the companies in the portfolio of the National Investment Company (SNI) apply the "**assisted* strategy",** which differs from that of **daddy's son*** in that, although their fields of activity are considered uncompetitive and of uncertain viability, the State grants them subsidies to keep them artificially breathing.

This means that companies' difficulties can come from strategic choices, management styles or poor market targeting.
The other constraint of the Cameroonian company is its inability to fully use its equipment.

3. THE UNDER-UTILISATION OF INSTALLED INDUSTRIAL CAPACITIES

Regardless of the size of the companies, many fail to optimize the use of their hard-earned capacities. Food industries are the first to be affected due to uncertainty in their supply of local or imported inputs, and poor referral to promising markets. In the construction sector, the dysfunctions of the public procurement system and the underutilization of investment credits penalize bidding companies by preventing the appropriate use of their logistics.

Table 26: Use of industrial capacities installed in 2010

	SIZE OF THE COMPANY	NUMBER OF ENTERPRISES	RATE OF UTILIZATION OF PRODUCTION CAPACITY
Type of enterprise	VSE	293	43 %
	SE	253	47 %
	ME	296	72 %
	LE	80	68 %
Sub-sectors	Extracting	16	87 %
	Food industries	177	57 %
	Other manufacturing industries	412	64 %
	Electricity	31	64 %
	Construction	286	31 %
Total		922	59%

Source: NIS/GEC 2009

The VSEs and SEs identified fail to use half of their installed capacity; large companies, including the extractive industries, do better than all others.

The disturbing question is therefore the following: what happens to the 36% of unused production capacity in the electricity, gas and water sub-sectors, which, although subject to costly investment, cannot meet demand. In the same context, a survey conducted on behalf of UNIDO by Samuel NOUMSI and Jean Claude TEKEU (2001) on' 'The Industrial Dimension of Sustainable Development in Cameroon," reveals the structural weaknesses of the country's industry, with ageing production equipment reaching more than 62% of the 500 units surveyed.

4. INDUSTRIAL SUBCONTRACTING ASSISTED BY ADMINISTRATIVE MEASURES

Subcontracting is a strategy by which a company delegates to another (very often an SME), a function (production, management, accounting, financing, logistics, marketing, sales, human resources), a part of its production or the production of certain components of its intermediate or final product. The subcontractor undertakes to carry out a part or a task on the basis of the instructions from the ordering company, which retains control over the product and its characteristics.

Subcontracting thus allows the contracting company to increase its flexibility and concentrate its resources on activities that it considers most strategic: competition policy and penetration of contestable markets, positioning in niches or markets sheltered by quantitative or qualitative barriers, planning, programming and synchronization of supplies.

Global, multinational, international or transnational firms very often decide to reduce their activities by contracting with other companies recognized for their expertise in a field, input or fragment of the main activity. They therefore outsource certain functions in a highly integrated global network. This practice is common in complex technology industries such as automotive and aeronautics.

In these industries, entire segments of the activity are delegated to sub-equipment manufacturers installed in a globalized network and coordinated by the client. Generally, the order for the seats is executed by Italian companies, and very often the accounting. The IT or electronics part is subcontracted to Japanese firms, while marketing can be located in London or Dubai, the finance function in Geneva, human resources in Madrid, logistics in the Netherlands, France, while some of the metal, chemical or technological equipment can come from Germany and the United States. China, India, Brazil, Israel, Russia, Argentina, South Africa and many other emerging countries are participating in these efforts to achieve productive efficiency and optimization on a global scale. It is a new IDL (International Division of Labor).

Legally, the subcontractor is different from the supplier in that the latter is fully responsible for the product or service he offers to his customer.

Thus, the widespread idea that globalized companies carrying out structuring projects in developing countries must transfer a fraction of their activity to domestic SMEs is economically incomprehensible insofar as it is not an act of generosity. These SMEs have the obligation to reach the IDL and to prove their ability to carry out part of the inputs (which are their outputs) of a technologically complex project under quality guarantee and according to an agreed timetable.

The Subcontracting Exchange as agreeable and politically attractive idea is implemented at the cost of many negotiations. The question is not about deciding in the name of an idyllic economic inclusion, to impose on large companies to reserve an activity quota for local SMEs. This is probably feasible for the recruitment of management staff. The main reason for a firm is not to create work for other companies, but to maximize profit for its shareholders. However, in its cost-minimization strategy, the firm can identify certain tasks that it can outsource and have them done, without this being a political calculation, a diplomatic or administrative arrangement.

This would be of poor service to domestic companies whose connection to the global company must be justified by their mastery of technological processes.

It is also common for SMEs to be created on the basis of the opportunities that they can offer large companies (LEs) that have set up or major government projects and as such target and negotiate subcontracting offers in areas of their specialty for which they have a competitive advantage. On the other hand, if these SMEs are created on an opportunistic basis while waiting for government support to obtain a share of the activity of these firms, they will become a problem instead of a solution to competitiveness, value creation and managerial efficiency.

As a problem, they will cause inertia and inefficiencies that prevent LEs from meeting contract deadlines and also product quality. Of course, these SMEs that claim their share in the activity will be missing in the technology transfer process for knowledge-intensive projects.

As a result, they may specialize in activities that are undervalued and without real prospects, such as those of sand delivery workers or food sellers near major construction sites.

Since the LE is responsible for the quality of the final product, SME subcontractors must provide guarantees to know the architecture of an industry, its processes, sub-activities and final products. It is on this basis that they position themselves by demonstrating their capabilities and performance.

Of course, it is socially or morally incomprehensible that large investments are made in a country without providing work for the SME. That's not the issue. The question is whether the local industrial base is able to seize opportunities and establish itself without jeopardizing the performance of the contracting firm.

Jean Pierre ANGELIER points out that: "the individual interests of firms do not necessarily correspond to those of the economy as a whole. This is why the intervention of public authorities is always necessary in order to ensure that the economic and social coherence on which the entire national economy is based and maintained.[23]" This is what is happening in Cameroon, and data from the Ministry of SMEs indicates that more than CFAF 76 billion in turnover was generated by subcontracting companies in 2017. However, it is impossible to know on what potential, at what price, neither too the value added produced, nor the corresponding profit margins.

CONCLUSION

The co-piloting of the industrial apparatus by the State and the private sector makes it essential to reformulate industrial policy in Cameroon; the aim being to stimulate the management of technical infrastructure and skills, to develop a business culture worthy of being taught in school and university cycles. Heroes and Business Angels would also be celebrated for their Success Stories.

The industrial dream will then be carried by the Vision of Emergence, but before addressing it, it is necessary to revisit the context that prevailed in the Cameroonian productive system before the formulation of this vision.

---

[23] Angelier, J. P (1991): Economie Industrielle. Eléments de méthode ; Presses Universitaires de Grenoble.

CHAPTER IV:

THEORETICAL FRAMEWORK

1. A SYNOPSIS OF INDUSTRIAL MODELS AND INSTRUMENTS

From the summary review of the industrial policies of the countries or groups of countries presented above, the "**German model"** has proven to be the most strategically and operationally complete design, and probably the most sophisticated in its architecture.

Based on the solidity and effectiveness of triangular State-Bank-Industry relations, this design allows for a deepening of social dialogue and the fight against inequality through income redistribution. The diversity and performance of its insurance system for workers guarantees industrial job security. The consensus sought in a triangular approach minimizes the risk of conflict, facilitates the detection of dysfunctions or the assessment of *orthofunctioning*, anticipation of results and timely strategic or managerial reviews. Economic and social efficiency is at the centre of this process, as is the coordination of intra- and inter-sector synergies. The coherence of government action is assessed in the allocation of multiform aid to SMEs in Länder.

Support for "National Champions" is part of the "**French Model"**. The French State provides strategic and financial support to companies that distinguish themselves in their results, their potential to create wealth and jobs, and that have proven managerial skills. Companies applying for the "national championship" in their branch or sector are expected to structure the productive sphere by satisfying the domestic market, exporting, disseminating subcontracting opportunities and positive technological or financial externalities. Success stories are celebrated at the national, regional or local level; as well as the promotion of innovative SMIs/SMEs and successful Start Ups.

The **"Italian Model"** on its part is characterized by its anchoring in the creation and accessibility of industrial basins thanks to heavy works for regional development. Italian industrial development policies at local level are based on flexible incentives and various facilities for SMEs. Horizontal strategic coordination by decentralized authorities of industrial and commercial dynamics helps to ensure the effectiveness of public-private partnerships.

Great Britain has taken the option of technological policies for SMEs. It is a unique and difficult experience of imitation by countries that do not create the industrial production tool and are limited with technology transfers that are sometimes outdated.

The important role of universities as promoters of centres of industrial excellence is a good example of the industrial version of the **American Way of Life**; but there is also the renewal of the debate on industrial policies during electoral cycles at both the federal and state levels. The use of public wealth to support industry is a thorny issue for crisis recovery in the USA, as it was the case in 2008 under Barack OBAMA's administration. The return to competitiveness of the automotive sector required huge subsidies repayable to the federal budget. It rehabilitated the job destroyed by a banking crisis caused by mortgage loans.

Japan's view is similar to the United States with regard to the industrial policy debate, but stands out as this debate is permanent (not only during the elections), partisan and uncompromising. Japan excels in reducing ministerial portfolios, concentrating governance and prominent responsibilities on a single department, MITI, responsible for the Economy, Finance, Industry and Technology. This scheme contributes to improving visibility throughout the economy and minimizes coordination and supervision difficulties, but the condition is that there must be a good and honest leadership, technically competent politicians to manage complex structures and be accountable to voters. The issue of social responsibility is therefore very important in this Empire, resulting in governmental instability and the succession of Prime Minister at a rate unimaginable in other countries.

It appears from the brief review of these experiences that the propensity to support SMEs is shared by the majority of developed countries, each one using the elements from its culture and background. Even more consensually, territorialized and horizontal policies are practiced in all developed and emerging countries. Everywhere, except Great Britain, and the USA to a certain extent, the State remains the master of the industrial game. To this end, the fate of governments in democratic countries largely depends on economic performance and particularly on industrial competitiveness. It is therefore up to each country to design its course.

2. ADVOCACIES FOR THE CAMEROON INDUSTRIALIZATION DISPUTES

Industrialization is far from being an isolated subject as public authorities, politicians, investors, experts/consultants, academics, researchers; civil society actors are all showing some concern. The questioning of Cameroon's industrialization came up at various levels of authority, but the eloquence of its defenders and accusations from sceptics did not allow for a final decision.

For OUMAROU SANDA: "the lateness in Cameroon's industrialization has several causes that can be attributed to both the State and the private sector: the choice of industries that are less growth-bearing, weak in local content and not very labour-intensive. They conveyed **a fake competitiveness** based on an increasingly outdated protectionism. By mimicry and lack of vision, the private sector reproduced the same approach as the State on the scale of investment[24]". To this, Mr SANZOUANGO, added: "Cameroon industrial companies are faced with several handicaps, chief among them being the organization, production, sales, logistics, quality, which have sealed competitiveness and deteriorated their confidence towards new global competition. These handicaps have also created rigidities, nostalgia for protectionism, reluctance to export, misunderstandings with the banking sector[25]". According to Mr ABANDA KPAMA (2009), "we act by mimicry and intuition. Many SME managers do not always have sufficient skills and experience to manage the companies they are promoting." Most worrisome is the noticeable of not being surrounded by qualified people. All the major industrial projects carried out in Cameroon so far excluded Cameroon SMEs from subcontracting, and the slightest transfer of technology avoided at all costs.

Cyrille BERTON accused "the cultural environment which, given the obstacles related to the physical and legal

---

[24] Sanda, O. (2002), Managing Director of Amity Bank Cameroon, in an interview with GICAM Quarterly Review.

[25] Sanzouango (2002), Secretary General of the Cameroon Employers Association and Editor-in-Chief of the GICAM Bulletin; Information Quarterly, No. 22, September 2002.

environment in particular, often favoured the search for an immediate return on investment rather than the long-term profitability specific to industrial projects[26]".

On the issue of the institutional environment, ABANDA KPAMA confirmed that: "the former structures for supervising and supporting SMEs have disappeared, thanks to IMF and the World Bank. FOGAPE, CAPME, FONADER, CDB were sacrificed on the altar of Structural Adjustment Program (SAPs). Those among the companies which have been resisting are barely surviving; and are wishing for "discussions on their governance to take place[27]". For Simon Maxime BIKOUE, "import substitution industrialization has been a failure for Africa because it made companies very uncompetitive, and did not help reduce imports. Instead, it changed their structure[28] ". His proposals were among others, based on technological control, foreign direct investment, tariff protection for infant industries, exports of manufactured goods to the world market and coordination of meso and macroeconomic policies. He also recommended limiting industrial policy to a few flexible actions of support and radically new productive combinations such as new materials, new energies and ICT. In "Globalisation et Diversification dans l'Appareil Industriel du Cameroun (Globalization and Diversification in Cameroon's Industrial Apparatus)", Georges Bertrand TAMOKWE PIAPTIE (2004) observed that "the agro-industrialization process was carried out in the form of technology transfer which took the form of high-risk investments and truncated joint

---

[26] CyrilleBerton, former Director of the French Development Agency.
[27].Sanzouango, op cit.
[28] Bikoue (6/10/05), Lecturer at the University of Douala, speaking at the CODESRIA General Assembly in Maputo on "The Problem of Industrialisation of Africa, the Need for Reformulation".

ventures[29]". It provided a diversity of information on Cameroon's attempts for industrialization and described investment choices that have resulted in gross failures when companies were technically and financially profitable. These companies, considered as Cameroon industry flagships, experienced unexpected events due to lobbies' war, the trading economy lurking in the shadows of bureaucrats, whose concessions had caused an irreversible human and financial waste, thus raising high barriers against the access of global competitiveness. Despite the assistance of multilaterals (World Bank, International Bank for Reconstruction and Development, European Investment Bank, European Development Fund) and bilateral (Central Fund for Economic Cooperation, Aid and Cooperation Fund, National Bank of Paris, Chase Manhattan Bank), technical and financial partners, Cameroon could not avoid being downgraded to Highly Indebted Poor Countries (HIPC) status. The opportunity costs caused by the renunciation of more profitable alternative investments for debt repayment have severely weakened industrial drivers and pillars, and affected investment capacity. The case of CELLUCAM is symptomatic of the pseudo-industrialization orchestrated by external assistance structures with which the national bureaucratic elite had often been an accomplice. According to G. B. Tamokwe, the venture which development economists described as a **"white elephant", "turnkey" factory**, was an operation where the plant was almost entirely dependent on imported chemical and technological inputs, to which could be added significant financial charges and technical assistance[30] '.

---

[29] .Tamokwé Paptie G. B. (2004): "Globalization and Diversification in Cameroon's Industrial Apparatus). PhD thesis in Economics, University of Douala, 2003-2004.

[30] Tamokwe Op cit.

In total, more than 120 billion CFA francs of investment gone up in smoke and the CELLUCAM dream lasted only two years after commissioning. Nearly three thousand people lost their jobs. What followed was nothing short of a nightmare and decades of irreparable economic, ecological, social and financial damages.

In terms of industrial restructuring, Cameroon had therefore not succeeded, like Algeria, in putting public companies in competition with each other. Algeria had succeeded in the challenge of resilience, by creating 103 companies through strategic segmentation from ashes of 18 others that had gone bankrupt.

CONCLUSION

Cameroon's specialization in the production of primary goods had often led to unstable gains in productivity that have been poorly spread in the economy, while prices of imported goods have continued to rise, leading to serious asymmetries in terms of trade. At the same time, producer prices have become random if not constantly fluctuating, leading to impoverishing growth. Cameroon remained trapped in the international division of labour in which it could, at best, remain a supplier of natural resources and cultivable land, all in a system with complex rigidity it could not control. At worst, it endured an expropriation of production resources such as the high-level expertise of its executives who left the country because of a poor salary package. Jane Jacobs' (1969) point of view constituted an appeal to remain positive as she states: "In my opinion, the fundamental conflict in the economy is between people whose interests are linked to already well-established activities and those whose interests are linked to the emergence of new economic activities[31]". G. Gilder

[31] George Gilder, op cit. p.249

specified that: “This does not concern the break-up between capitalists and workers, technocrats and humanists, governments and companies, liberal and conservative, or rich and poor. All these divisions are partial and distorted reflections of a more fundamental conflict: the struggle between the past and the future, between the existing configuration of companies and the industries that will one day replace them[32]”.

[32] Ditto

CHAPTER V:

COMPETITIVENESS AT STAKE IN CAMEROON

Overview of Industrial Activity on the Eve of the Formulation of the Vision

Table 27: Nominal turnover (in CFAF billions) and number of employees of companies

TYPE OF INDUSTRY	Number of Enterprises	Turnover	Number of Employees	Female Staff
Extractive industries	25	434.3	1,162	209
Food, beverages and tobacco	695	593.9	19,447	4,239
Textiles clothing, leather and shoes	6,387	99.1	14,162	4,856
Wood, paper, printing and publishing	1,084	235.1	12,043	1,378
Chemistry, refining, rubber, plastic	92	1,177	10,481	1,424
Construction material, metalworking, foundries	184	129.0	1,756	118
Metal structures, electrical appliances and transport equipment	880	310.7	6,808	1,974
Other manufacturing industries	1,600	30.0	4,743	400
Electricity, gas and water	74	275.0	8,530	2,152
Construction	664	228.2	8,757	1,368
Total	11,685	3,502	87 889	18,118

Source: NIS/GEC 2009

Table 28: Distribution of companies by source of capital in 2008

TYPE OF ENTERPRISE	SHARE CAPITAL					
	Mostly Cameroonian		Mostly foreign		Non-declared	
	Number of enterprises	Number of employees	Number of enterprises	Number of employees	Number of enterprises	Number of employees
VSE	9,733	19,898	166	683	18	34
SE	562	3,403	39	421	192	1,106
ME	370	3,274	50	1,403	295	4,460
LE	110	19,616	80	23,837	70	7,754
Total	10,775	48,191	335	26,344	575	13,354

Source: NIS/GEC 2009

Mathematically, "92% of industrial companies belong to Cameroonians but 90.3% are very small businesses. More than half of these units are in the textile and clothing industry. In addition, industries with a majority of Cameroonian's capital employ 54.8% of the workforce compared to 30% for companies controlled by foreigners[33]".

Another revelation in the period before 1997 was that "the longevity of companies with a majority of Cameroonian capital is twice as long as that of foreign companies. Since 1997, a relatively stable period, the survival of Cameroonian-owned companies seems high and has become comparable to that of production units made on foreign capital[34]".

The longevity levers are not explained in the survey. It might be determined either by the improving economic profitability, management control, or barriers to exit from certain industries.

[33] NIS/GEC 2009, p.73.
[34] NIS/GEC 2009, p.74.

Table 29: Evolution of industrial employment

YEAR SECTOR	2003	2004	2005	2006	2007	AVERAGE
1. Agro-industry	33,268	33,055	33,602	34,573	36,837	34,267.0
2. Forest	3,162	2,116	2,395	2,395	2,481	2,509.8
3. Energy/water resources	5,783	6,024	5,567	5,630	6,019	5,804.6
4. Food	1,727	1,725	1,930	2,130	2,500	2,002.4
5. Beverages/ tobacco	3,216	3,436	2,544	2,527	2,598	2,864.2
6. Textile/leather	1,336	1,154	941	943	956	1,066.0
7. Paper, plastic	821	670	611	665	587	670.8
8. Chemistry	899	498	490	391	315	518.6
9. Cement/ metalworking	1,505	1,431	1,506	1,501	1,500	1,488.6
Industrial sector	51,717	50,109	49,586	50,755	53,793	51,192.0

Source: ETC /GICAM

The trend in industrial employment is generally sluggish, with the number of employees falling to around 51,000 (including temporary jobs). As a result, the industrial sector creates few jobs; it lost a lot of them in 2005. Food industry is characterized by a very high number of jobs (65% on average in the industrial sector), hard work and low wages.

Although the country produces oil, Chemicals seems to be a declining sector with a 64% decrease in employment in four years. The Paper and Plastics sector is facing uncertain prospects. On the other hand, the agro-industry, water and energy sectors are potentially growth-generating; meeting the deadlines for the commissioning of new energy infrastructure is a real challenge.

Table 30: Evolution of exports of some products of the local industry (in millions FCFA)

Products	2003	2004	2005	2006	2007
Food preparations and others	12,311.1	6,567.1	1,858.6	4,887.9	7,124.9
Beer and fizzy drink	4,684.1	2,807.8	1,625.6	1,515.3	4,858.9
Cotton fabric	957.0	469.0	3386	132.5	147.1
Electric batteries and others	2,275.0	781	706	1,629.0	889.2

Source: NIS, Foreign Trade Statistics, 2008.

Agro-industry employs 67.9% of the workforce (mainly temporary and young people) in the industrial sector, and pays 33.7% of the wage bill.

According to NIS; "Since 2000, GDP growth has been driven mainly by the tertiary sector and, since 2007, by the latter and the agricultural sector. The evolutions are in the whole extremely moderate amplitudes, ranging between 2% and 4%"[35].

1. THE BREAKDOWNS IN THE LEVERS OF COMPETITIVENESS

The bankruptcy of the main support mechanisms for industrial project leaders: FONADER, FOGAPE, BCD, CAPME, Centre National du Commerce Extérieur (CNE), Crédit Agricole du Cameroun (CAC), Office National de Commercialisation des Produits de Base (ONCPB), has contributed to fundamentally changing the technical and financing offer of the Cameroonian industry. The mortality that has affected public companies in the productive sector

[35] NIS/GEC 2009, p.71.

has also led to the collapse of the banking system, the restructuring of which will cost the State, companies and households dearly; and even the recovered health of some banking institutions as a result of painful reforms has not been accompanied by a desire to make up for lost opportunities. On the contrary, DIY and reluctance to grant production loans have become widespread and banks have become loaded with excess liquidity in an economy under liquidity stress; and they boast about it.

By refusing to take risks, investment banks have turned to short-term credit: 85% of the amounts granted, including 40% for general distribution and export trade. Industrial projects benefit from short, inadequate credits, often with distant or uncertain profitability. Long-term financing mainly benefits large telecommunications projects, which account for nearly 50% of the volume.

The agricultural sector receives 10% of short-term credits; but the total supply of credits (short, medium and long term) remains very low compared to demand. However, according to the Food and Agriculture Organization (FAO), each state must allocate 25% of the national budget to agriculture. In Cameroon, this rate is barely 8% in terms of allocations; disbursements are another matter.

Table 31: Evolution of the bank credit offer to the rural sector

SECTIONS (Amounts In Thousands C FAF)	2001		2002		2003		2004	
	Amount	% of total credit	Amount	% of total credit	Amount	% of total credit	Amount	% of total credit
Agriculture production	81,664	6.6	88,216	6.8	82,374	5.8	81,976	5.5
Unprocessed production	17,266	1.4	21,037	1.6	20,139	1.4	15,961	1.1
-First stage processing Agricultural products	27,351	2.2	28,517	2.2	22,610	1.6	25,829	1.7
Agriculture appendices	37,048	3.0	38,660	3.0	39,625	2.8	40,186	2.7
Livestock products	1,116	0.09	1,603	0.12	930	0.07	2,118	0.14
Fishing production	4,209	0.34	4,727	0.37	4,853	0.34	4,813	0.32
Sector total	86,990	7.06	94,547	7.30	88,166	6.23	88,907	5.98

NIS/GEC 2009

Trends towards stagnation and even contraction in the volume of credit granted to rural sector production are confirmed. Amounts allocated to agro-pastoral and fisheries activity are derisory compared to the important national and sub-regional market to be satisfied; hence the need to create financing mechanisms capable of vigorously supporting this sector, which could potentially create jobs and value. The depth of the sectors, the width of the product ranges and the diversity of the professions to be promoted are real incentives. Also, in view of the massive imports of mass consumption foodstuffs such as rice and vegetable oils, the winning strategy would be to allocate massive financing to reverse the trend and get repositioned as a net exporter of these products to major local markets such as Nigeria and the Democratic Republic of Congo (DRC).

Table 32: Structure of the GDP (%)

FORMULATION	**1993 - 1994**	**1995 - 1999**	**2000 - 2004**	**2004 - 2009**
Primary sector	20.4	20.2	20.3	20.9
Secondary sector	36.1	32.8	31.1	26.6
Tertiary sector	27.2	29.3	32.7	35.8
Non-market GDP	9.2	8.6	8.8	9.1
Total GDP	**100.0**	**100.0**	**100.0**	**100.0**

Source: NIS National accounts.

The GDP of the primary sector is generated 64% by agriculture, 18% by forestry and 15% by livestock. The rural sector accounts for 30% of foreign exchange earnings, a proportion that could increase if the Rural Sector Strategy were rigorously implemented.

Globally, 90.33% of Cameroonian companies are VSEs, which employ 41% of the workforce, just like large firms (GEs), which account for only 1% of the total. These large companies, 80% controlled by international capital, provide one and a half times more jobs than the 9,733 VSEs and seven times more than the 370 SMEs surveyed. A large business park was created at the end of the first decade of the 21st century, thanks to the administrative facilities put in place. Almost half (46%) of the industrial turnover is generated by only two branches: - extractive industries (12.4%), - oil refinery (33.6%), activities considered highly capital intensive and extroverted.

Sectorial bank financing, whose network and windows remain limited, is highly discriminatory, with preference given to agricultural projects, to the detriment of those in the livestock and fisheries sectors, despite their proven profitability.

Major Constraints to Competitiveness in Heavy Industry

It was noted in 2007 that the implementation of the measures under the IMF-supported three-year PRGF (Poverty Reduction and Growth Facility) programme did not achieve the desired level of performance. This failure is due to the investment that were not programmed and to the lack of precision in the conduct of reforms. In a context of economic gloom, it was noted that:

- the primary sector experienced uncontrolled fluctuations;
- the secondary sector lacked benchmarks and was deteriorating sharply;
- the tertiarization of the economy that has begun is poorly managed and loses opportunities.

Donors have insistently criticized:

- Poorly prepared and conducted privatizations;
- The low competitiveness of companies;
- The low level of banking intermediation coupled with a low rate of banking;
- The inadequacy of the infrastructure network, particularly in terms of energy.

In total, the Cameroonian economy did not produce any power capable of propelling strong growth, as the levers identified were little or no exploited. According to donors, these poor economic performances are due to the inability and incompetence of the administration to stimulate the economic machine to achieve vigorous and sustainable growth. This proven or assumed inability is recurrent in the analysis of the rates of completion of investments from all consolidated sources of financing.

2. CAMEROON IN A WEAK POSITION

Local mineral processing in developing countries is a problem that resists solution trials; the cause is that mining companies, which are generally triadic and true oligopolies integrated upstream, have no desire to diversify downstream. The decision to relocate processing to mining sites is part of a more global policy that is not simply a matter of the profitability of individual mining projects, let alone the desire of the countries that own the deposits.

Fundamentally, the strategy of firms in this sector is to increase their size, competitiveness, resistance to economic shocks such as stock market fluctuations, fluctuations in economic activity (short- and medium-term elasticity of supply and demand) focused on the triad (Western Europe, North America, South and East Asia), as well as technological change. It is in fact a question of seeking the maximum power that corresponds to the critical dimension from which they can influence the competitive game, in international negotiations or with the public authorities of mineral-owning countries, and take advantage of possible conflicts. The search for economies of scale is also a massive argument for these firms, whose tendency is to raise barriers to entry into the industry and whose aim is to control all segments of the economic process.

Yves MORVAN gives his point of view on this issue: “Sector and vertical integration policies push dominant firms to control various stages of the economic process, so as to internalize many functions and reduce current and potential competition[36]”.

This is a way of protecting against sudden supply disruptions, as was the case with oil in 1973 and 1979-80.

---

36 Morvan, Y. (1991),"Fondements de l'Economie Industrielle", Paris, 2nd Edition, page 154.

With his style, René DUMONT comments on this subject: “thus reserving first-class metallurgical deposits for itself is a new form of capitalist robbery. All profits are, as with oil, in processing and not in mining. The context of Africa-France-Europe relations prevents the emergence of real development poles capable of driving the entire economy of the Black Continent[37]”.

The Poor Quality of Local Expertise

The development of heavy industry has been bumpy in Cameroon due to the lack of technological, human, financial, energy and infrastructure capacities. It is therefore difficult to take shortcuts in a field as complex as the steel industry.

The National School of Administration and Magistracy (ENAM) was created in 1959 before taking an interest in engineering and technical schools. It was the great clerks from these moulds who developed the doctrine that inspired politicians, some of whom came from their ranks! Robert BARRO argues that “public spending on education, R&D, transport and communication infrastructure is directly productive and must be considered as one of the factors of the production function[38]”. The American industrialist Henry Ford was just as intractable on this subject: “The two most important assets of a company are not its balance sheet; they are its people and reputation[39]”,

"The unique resource of companies that have survived all the perils and are flying towards tomorrow’s victories is the human resource. Every man is capable of inventing, of imagining. There is no millenary fatality in the rhythms of

[37] Dumont, René, Op.cit.

[38] Barro R. J. (2000), The Factors of Economic Growth, Economica.

[39] Henry Ford, quoted by Christine Drullion in, “The NGOs: New Sentinels for the Reputation of Enterprises”

nature. Developing countries can skip all the stages of the 19th and 20th centuries, thanks to the new challenges of science. Today, the workforce we are looking for is the one that is capable, through continuous training, of mastering new technologies and advanced knowledge[40]".

To strengthen its scientific and technical knowledge base, Cameroon should create very elitist engineering schools, a mix of French, Chinese, American, Japanese, Indian, British and Brazilian experiences would provide a good mix in terms of training and specialization.

The Curse of Raw Materials as a Challenge for Emergence

Cameroon's natural factor endowments are not fully identified and those that are remaining under-exploited. According to François Chesnais (1997): "Countries whose integration into world trade took place during the era of open colonial or semi-colonial domination as exporters of primary agricultural or mining products have been particularly affected by commodity substitution that destroys trade flows[41]; this is the case of Cameroon. And the author adds: "Everything converges so that these countries remain prisoners of specializations made obsolete by the evolution of scientific knowledge and technologies accumulated by advanced countries[42].

Furthermore, he says: "As former colonized countries, heirs of state apparatus created by the tutelary power, endowed with ruling elites trained in the school of

---

[40] Pisar Samuel: La Ressource Humaine (1983)

[41] Chesnais. F., (1997): ''the Globalization of the Capital''; New Added Edition; Alternatives Economiques; SYROS.

[42] Ditto

parasitism and corruption, they are practically defenceless against such developments[43]".

Will the instrumentation of the process of catching up with the industrial backlog be supported by the cross-fertilization of knowledge, skills and experience on open or imaginable projects so that Cameroon can enter the global economy by following its own trajectories? Things do not seem to be so easy; hence the inevitable and scary question is whether, given its many and rich deposits, Cameroon is currently in a position to start a competitive heavy industry, particularly the steel industry?

Geopolitical Asymmetries in the Mining Industry

The economic order in which mining resources are developed is at the core of the International Labour Division (ILD), which is marked by structural rigidities: location of production and trade. Thus, Cameroon's desire to *de-specialize* raw minerals and set up processing capacities (smelteries, rolling mills, refineries) is hampered by the realities inherent in the nature of this globally structured industry. Notably, the location of mineral processing industries is not solely the will of the mine owner; it is faced with speculation from metallurgical companies, which are often in a monopoly or oligopoly position. Overall, the strategy of developing countries to build capacity to process a larger proportion of their minerals has gradually emerged over time. The United Nations Conference on Trade and Development, UNCTAD IV (Geneva 1975), presented this subject as one of the main axes of industrialization to be favoured in developing countries; but the realization of this intention did not follow.

---

[43] Ibidem.

Discriminatory Exploitation of the Minerals in a Deposit: An Obstacle to Competitiveness

Legally, mineral deposits are the property of the State and are part of its strategic domain. Research and mining agreements are concluded between the State and companies, which are required to apply its Mining Regime. And yet, things are different. The role of public authorities in guiding mining development, taking into account fiscal, social and environmental sustainability, is hampered by the natural complexity of deposits and by technical and financial barriers erected by global firms. It should therefore be noted that sands containing ores are often polymetallic, i.e. composed of complementary or competing metals from an industrial or commercial perspective.

In Cameroon, the rutile deposits also contain ilmenite and zircon, all three titanium ores, which can be extracted by the same technical process and for identical or complementary industrial applications. The same applies to the alternative choice between cobalt and nickel. Chromium, zinc, manganese, tin, iron, aluminium, copper..., are very often found in the same mining basin, at different concentration rates. In these cases, the decision to exploit an ore rests with the transnational firm that holds the processes, capital and considerable bargaining power. The control of processing stages, the market value of intermediate or final products, and marketing channels are almost entirely beyond the control of the Owner State.

As a result, it is difficult for it, in the absence of appropriate verification tools and expertise, to control or audit the exclusive exploitation of an ore whose process is inevitably linked or not to another. Moreover, the fate of the ore whose extraction is deferred is also a matter of concern. Consequently, the sovereign objective that the State sets for itself to stimulate mining research and development on its territory in order to be free from global groups is subject to the harsh geo-economic reality. It is in this context of external appropriation of heritage that opportunity and transaction costs arise because the State is not in control of the industrial game and, in particular, that relating to the mining sector.

In the current state of global industrial governance, this sector, which is reputed to be intensive in terms of technological, financial and infrastructural resources, is developing asymmetries and the eviction power of the owners of their mining sites, to the benefit of the operators. These abuses are eloquently analysed by A. CHIENG (1989): "States seek to protect themselves from the excesses that have resulted from ancient forms of mining: holding concessions for very long periods, insufficient exploration, withholding information on discoveries made, exclusive exploitation of the richest deposits, considerable loss of profits due to the undervaluation of exports and the overvaluation of inputs import". Also, "the low training efforts of local staff, the low local added value and the refusal to carry out processing on site, even if it is economically justified".

On-Site Processing or Export of Raw Ore?
A Binary Vision In Favour of Multinationals

The metals market is generally a highly concentrated "oligopsone" downstream because mining processing companies fear supply disruptions that can lead to very high marginal costs on purchases. In this logic, the firms involved prefer to negotiate the value retained in terms of salaries, taxes and duties, expenses incurred by the use of infrastructure and factor services (water, electricity, telephone, and transport). However, the producing country believes that it could improve its capacity to capture benefits and its impact on rents if the processing infrastructure were to develop near the mining basin.

The argument put forward by nationals is that the export of processed products improves the external balance; but this does not take into account the fact that on-site smelting and refining is only possible at the cost of heavy and costly imports of essential mining inputs and equipment, the expenditure of which is likely to cancel out expected rents. It should also be considered that the supply of mining inputs is in some cases accompanied by debt on the financial and banking markets that burden the results of the national or nationalized company. This means that the issue of mining transformation should not be analysed on the basis of a cautious nationalism, but in view of national, sectorial or global issues, and the impacts on trade, society and the environment. For this reason, it is quite understandable that the country that owns the resource claims the right to control the downstream end of the chain. However, entry into the mining industry is not on a heritage or sentimental basis. Many financial and scientific barriers exist or can appear in each segment of the process and siphon off all the gains expected by the State. René Dumont thinks on this subject that: "With its natural resources, it would be possible to produce in Africa - at rationally selected points - hundreds of tons of metals. The huge investments that this requires would risk being wasted if each state wanted to own its own heavy industry to satisfy its desire for prestige. The blast furnaces and steel mills of tropical Africa will require, operating economically, cheap energy, a fairly large market, trained technicians, and transporting of non-prohibitive raw materials".

CONCLUSION

The problem of the alternative choice of minerals to be exploited from a polymetallic deposit is a matter of international industrial economics, geopolitics and geo-economics. Knowledge of these global logics makes it possible to avoid romantic or political analyses developed by nation-states; hence EKANI ONAMBÉLÉ's observation: "the first major lesson is that the State bears an immense responsibility in underdeveloped countries in the struggle for economic and social development".

In the chronicles of Cameroon's economic history, we can note the recurrence of some programs:

1°) the access to electrical energy;

2°) the creation of communication and telecommunication infrastructures;

3°) the modernization of agricultural sectors;

4°) the industrial processing of local cash crops;

5°) the construction of social housing;

6°) The poverty reduction.

These programmes benefited from budgetary preferences in the hope that the expected multiplier effects would be disseminated to the economic and social community by creating opportunities and potential for the industrial investor. In the past, many things were tried or almost tried to reach the summit; but the rock came down each time at the foot of the mountain.

The vision of emergence can be seen as a breather for another start; this time, using new muscles and a different elixir to boost the actors involved in the success of this bet.

CHAPTER VI:

THE UNRESOLVED EQUATION OF THE PROJECTS FINANCING

The question is also to know what will generate the resources to finance these costly programmes, while the trend is for tax revenues to stagnate since 2012 and oil revenues to stagnate since 2015. External financing remains the ultimate solution; however, at this level too, there are obstacles and Cameroon cannot go back into debt as it wishes, regardless of the pressure of its needs.

The international financial community's debt management dates back to the completion point of the HIPC initiative in 2006. Conservatory measures are being taken to prevent the country from going back into debt in an unsustainable way.

Although the economic convergence criteria contained in CEMAC Regulation No. 12/07-UEAC-186-CM-15 of 19 March 2007 on the reference framework for debt policy and public debt management give the government considerable scope for negotiating new loans to finance its development, it must take into account the opinion of its parliament, both internally and externally, of international donors. Pursuant to the said regulation, Cameroon has already set up a National Committee on Public Debt to coordinate its policy in this area, in conjunction with other macroeconomic policies. The challenge is that this Committee should be free to operate independently, responsibly and professionally!

The debt strategy document now annexed to the Finance Bill requests the government to highlight:

a) The justification for the loan;
b) Debt ceilings and guarantees granted by the State;
c) The structure of the portfolio of new borrowings;
d) Indicative terms of borrowings;
e) The debt sustainability profile over a 15-year horizon.

Parliament is then called upon to agree (as if it had the latitude to do otherwise) to the government's willingness to take out new loans. Less pressure from the Executive is still an important step towards sincerity, transparency and democratic ownership of areas previously reserved for central government insiders.

However, the transition to the programme-budget since January 2013 is far from simplifying things for parliamentarians who do not always benefit from the cooperation of an administration reputed to be "Zen", arrogant and unmoved as long as its interests are not threatened.

The search for secure resources for investment will neither be spared from the possibility of economic and technological shocks, nor from the volatility of commodity and currency prices, let alone from industrial, social and political changes at the global, regional or national level.

Reflating the Banking Activity to Support Competitiveness

Before the crisis of the 1980s, the bank was the preferred financing mechanism for SMEs in Cameroon. Since then, things have changed with the disappearance of several banking and non-banking organizations. Conditions for access to credit have been tightened and a distance has gradually widened between bankers and their customers, two complementary players in the financial and industrial scene. From now on, loans are granted to SMEs on a short-term basis or, as part of the execution of the public procurement. And even in this context, risks are calculated and reflected in the interest rates charged.

Could Industrialization be funded by Official Development Assistance (ODA)?

The answer to this question requires a brief overview of the history of Official Development Assistance (ODA) and its involvement in a few industrial operations in Cameroon. Historically, colonial aid was already the subject of Adam Smith's criticisms, who devoted it about twenty pages in his book entitled "*The Wealth of the Nations*" published in 1776. For him and for the liberal economists, aid is a perverse transaction as an allocation of non-market resources; the market being considered as the only effective mechanism for coordinating agents and optimizing resource allocation. Development assistance was first allocated through the U.S programme of assistance to the citizens of Venezuela in 1812. Under pressure from producer lobbies, Americans used their agricultural surpluses in 1896 to help other countries that were struggling to fill their food deficits (HJERTHOLM and White, 2000). Donations of American rice, wheat and milk then travelled around the developing world. But it was only after the Second World War that the ODA apparatus has been structured, so the idea of international solidarity took shape. It was then guided by political and geostrategic interests during the 1950s and 1960s.The 1970s, 1990s and 2000s were marked by the moral obligation of developed countries in the North to assist those in the South in their efforts to reduce poverty and public debt. Thanks to the ideological, technical and financial framework of the World Bank and the International Monetary Fund, the Structural Adjustment and Economic Recovery Policies were implemented during the years 80s in over-indebted developing countries.

Debates on development assistance are numerous and often heated. For P.T. Bauer (1984), committed ideologue: "helping leaders based on the poverty of their people is more likely to encourage impoverishment policies than to hinder them".

This hostility towards aid is also reflected in the neo-Marxian analysis of development, which sees in ODA an instrument of the global reproduction of the relationship between central and peripheral exploitation, and a means of strengthening the dependence of countries in the South on those in the North. For Samir Amin, this dependence is due to the fact that aid is a bias in the sectorial allocation of investments at the same time as it favours activities that enhance the recipient country's integration into an imperialist-type International Division of Labour (IDL).

To situate ODA in its dialectical complexity, Jean Michel SEVERINO and Pierre JACQUET recall that: "Development assistance is the only true global public policy with a financial dimension, even if its implementation is, and remains, scattered among a large number of bilateral, multilateral or non-governmental actors. It is the result of the Second World War, decolonization and the Cold War[44]». But this does not prevent him from expressing some scepticism: "Refunding the legitimacy of this public policy by making it an instrument for managing globalization is not enough. Not only must its conceptual foundations be solid, but also its management methods must be effective[45]".

---

44 Severino J.M (2002) Ex Managing Director of the French Development Agency (AFD); Jacquet, P. (Chief economist at AFD): "development assistance, a public policy at the heart of sustainable development and the governance of globalization" Article published in the Revue de l'Economie Financière, n°66, 2002.
45 Ditto

At the doctrinal level, the direct channelling of ODA to industrial projects in recipient countries has been carefully avoided. However, it can be established that assistance granted to the infrastructure, agriculture, health and education sectors is considered to be indirectly targeted at industry. Cindy Williams thinks, it would not be possible, the issue is about: "helping a country's economy move beyond the stage where it was confined to consume its seeds. Most of the assistance to the poorest countries cannot even get them to go that far; it simply raises them to the level of a subsistence economy[46]". To overcome this, J-M SEVERINO and P. JACQUET propose that development aid should now aim at "ensuring financial and knowledge transfers and contributing to the creation of a legitimate governance of globalization, enabling it to achieve economic objectives that will make it sustainable".

From this point of view, stakeholders should rebuild aid in a perspective of economic and social progress and a balance in North-South relations. To this end, they should verify that the financing agreements under negotiation or in execution are accompanied by modalities for the transfer of knowledge or simply technology, to borrow from the established language. In this respect, the governance of development programme and projects should be concerned with the creation of value in industry and trade, impacting the economy in its process of connecting to a globalization that respects human rights. Otherwise, "our country will permanently remain outside the globalized economy and

---

[46] Cindy Williams, Deputy Director of the National Security Division, at the Congressional Budget Office: "Evaluation of the Impact of External Assistance on Development", article published in **Economic Outlook**, USA Electronic Review Volume 1, No. 11, August 1996. Excerpt from her presentation in May 1996 to the Senate Subcommittee on African Affairs on the role of external assistance in economic development.

thus limited to an economy of implementation" (Professor Georges NGANGO, 1990).

Public companies more generally, and quite often those in the private sector of Cameroon in the 1970s had received significant external transfers for on-lent or guaranteed debt. Unfortunately, the real or artificial insolvency of these second-tier borrowers contributed to the state's over-indebtedness during the 1980s.

The question of the absorption[47] of external aid was addressed in 2010 by a Think Tank, GPPi (Global Public Policy Institute). Other constraints considered as major exist, such as:

- The weakness of institutional and managerial capacities;
- The ineffective project planning and programming;
- Serious delays in acquisitions and infrastructure design defects;
- Legal uncertainty in case of disputes concerning public procurement.

All this conditioned the "capacity or inability to absorb", a somewhat simplistic and falsely pedantic expression, which trivialized a serious phenomenon of leadership and management. This term implied that development resources were intended for mechanical consumption.

The following table presents a sample of those companies which, due to their poor performance, had not succeeded in producing value within their operating process to help the State repay the debt incurred.

---

[47] "Analysis of the Factors Limiting Cameroon's Capacity to Absorb Foreign Aid", Report written by Jenny Sharer of the Cabinet Global Public Policy Institute (GPPi), (2010). Yaoundé.

Table 33: Investments (in billions of CFA francs) and jobs in certain industrial or agricultural industries complexes

COMPANIES	COST IN CFA FRANCS OF INVESTMENTS IN 10^9	NUMBER OF JOBS CREATED
SOCAME	30	380
CELLUCAM	75	2,200
ALUCAM	23.2	77
CAMSUCO	23.7	3,126
SODEBLE	10	500
SEMRY II	13.6	7000 (projected)
SONARA	66	302

Source: IDA, J. C. Willame[48].

One Example: the Wheat Development Company

The case of this company is pathetically described by Sophie BESSIS: "The investments required to launch SODEBLE in 1975 amounted to CFAF 10 billion. In 1978, only 100 hectares of wheat were harvested and yields did not exceed 200 kg/ha despite excessive mechanization, massive application of fertilizers... and the presence of 500 permanent employees in the company. In September 1988, the company had swallowed up huge sums of money for almost no results[49]".

These and other experiences had over-indebted Cameroon and sparked off a severe economic crisis. The accumulation of debts accelerated as early as 1975, as shown in the following table:

---

48 "The President of the International Development Association (IDA) report and recommendations to the Executive Directors". Report no. P-3074-CM, Washington, 1981. Quoted by J. C. Willame: In «*Cameroun, les Avatars du Libéralisme Planifié* ».

49 Bessis, S.:(Hunger around the world. REPERES; edited by La Découverte; p. 52.

Table 34: Evolution of external debt expressed in millions of US dollars

YEARS	IN PROGRESS	UNDISBURSED	TOTAL
1973	236.8	194.6	431.4
1975	371.7	321.1	692.8
1977	823.6	543.7	1,367. 3
1978	1,135.6	787.3	1922.9
1979	1,636.3	1,071.8	2,708.1
1980	1,998.7	612.5	2,611.2
1981	2,020.5	544.3	2,564.8
1982	1912.0	679.4	2,591.4
1983	2,260.8	1,106.6	3,367.4

Source: Jeune Afrique Economique No.56, Dec. 1984 edition.
At the end of 1983, 1 dollar = 417.1 F CFA.

In addition to the financial waste resulting from unproductive investments because they were clumsy and poorly managed, there was the social cost paid by the community, including thousands of families and workers from across the country. Several careers had broken down and uncertainty, coupled with the late release of compensation, had not allowed for professional retraining or the creation of new sources of income. For many, it was the end of a dream, and very often, of a life!

These examples, among many others, show to what extent Cameroon's industrialization paths with external funding are full of tragedies. So, things should be done differently. How then, as long as business governance is neither effective nor accountable?

The Sectorial Concentration of a Few Donors

Since 2006, the sectorial concentration of donors has become more and more precise. The main multilateral creditors (IMF, ADF, IDA, IDB, BADEA, OPEC Fund,

IFAD and EU) or bilateral creditors, members or not of the Paris Club (France, Belgium, Germany, Spain, the Netherlands, China, Kuwait and Saudi Arabia), do not operate directly in the industrial sector.

Table 35: Sectorial concentration of aid in billions CFA francs

TITLE OF THE SUB-SECTORS	PROGRAMMES/ PROJECTS	PERIOD	AMOUNT
Basic Education	8	2006- 2013	81.4
Health	10	2003- 2013	85.6
Water and Sanitation	11	2005- 2012	58.06
Good governance	13	2005- 2011	39.1
Support to Decentralization	5	2003, 2010	52.6
Energy	3	2008- 2013	65
Agriculture and Food Security	26	2004- 2010	81.6
Forestry and Environment	29	2002- 2014	113.5

Source: Sector-based matrix of the Multi-Donor Committee, 2009.

This ideologically marked decline of technical and financial partners in their preferred sectors can be managed in a highly profitable way if the Government takes strategic ownership of it. But the paradox lies in the use of aid disbursements, which are modestly referred to as "absorption capacity".

In November 2011, Cameroon had again crossed the CFAF 2,000 billion debt threshold, then 2,700 billion in 2014, while the disbursement and transformation rates of this debt were hardly improving. Many programmes and projects carried forward budget allocations over several years.

The slow disbursement of resources, coupled with the under-optimization of the use of funds received in a cash-stressed country like Cameroon, is simply incomprehensible and even disturbing.

Funding Industry through a Capital-Intensive Shock

Cameroon's economy is financed in a very monotonous way. Resources of budgetary origin are distributed with the constraint of not forgetting any sector, even if it means sprinkling them. Indirect financing of the industry through public debt and trust funds has a limited multiplier effect. The impact of capital spending is little felt on growth, which is struggling to reach the announced rates. It is therefore necessary to increase in severity on the financial scale through a massive use of alternative resources. So-called innovative, alternative or emerging financing is carried by institutional investors (pension funds, insurance companies), traditional banks, the State, and citizens through crowd funding.

The role of remittance mechanisms, microfinance institutions and telephone operators is extended to financial intermediation. The challenge for Cameroon is to optimize these financing methods, the functioning of which requires the provision of appropriate institutional, organizational, managerial, legal and technological skills.

More concretely, it will be a set of measures aimed at:

Increasing the Volume and Quality of Remittances from the Diaspora

According to the World Bank, remittances from the diaspora are the second largest foreign exchange resource in many African countries. A joint report by the African Development Bank (AfDB) and the World Bank (WB) revealed that "in 2010, the financial transfers to the continent of the 30 million Africans living outside their countries of origin reached 40 billion US dollars; which is comparable to the volume of foreign aid received each year by this continent most often, under very restrictive conditions".

Identified in the GESP as a source of financing for the economy, the increased mobilization of diaspora funds also appeared to be an area for improvement in the common transfer's stations. According to diplomatic and consular sources, the number of Cameroonian emigrants is estimated to at least 4,000,000 (four million), with the main concentrations being Nigeria (2,000,000), the United States (700,000), Gabon (50,000), France (40,000), Equatorial Guinea (16,000) and Germany (7,000).

From a financial point of view, the actual amount of remittances is still difficult to assess given the importance of informal transfers. However, WB (2009) data show an increase in the amount of Cameroonian remittances from abroad from USD 11 million in 2000 to 167 million in 2008. Although substantial, these flows (0.8% of GDP in 2008) compared to some African countries, remain very low. Transfers recorded in 2008 in Cameroon without institutional support still represented a third (33%) of customs revenues, 50% of multilateral and bilateral direct loans, and 75% of personal income tax; which represents an undeniable source of resources.

Improving the level of transfers would require a series of incentives to secure savings. To this end, measures should be taken to encourage the financial and banking sector, investment funds and investor groups to compete creatively in the intermediation and investment of these funds

BOX 1: diaspora transfers

> Assuming that 1,000,000 (25%) Cameroonians out of the 4,000,000 registered in the diaspora transfers 2,000 euros each to the country annually; this would correspond to 2 billion euros, or more than 1,300 billion CFA francs. This sum corresponds to 50% of the 2011 State budget, 16% of GDP, roughly the total of the budgets allocated to the three departments in charge of education, public works and public health.
>
> This objective requires institutional, strategic and operational support from the public authority to be achieved or exceeded, which provides guarantees in terms of security and country risk. The involvement of business lawyers, solicitors, notaries, financing entities, bankers, and investors would enhance the effectiveness of a system that generates skilled jobs.

Attracting Foreign Direct Investment (FDI)

Although accounting for 40% of the sub-region's economic weight in 2010, Cameroon attracts less than 15% of CEMAC's FDI. According to Bank of Central African States (BEAC) sources, the ratio of FDI per country in the sub-region between 2000 and 2006 is as follows: Cameroon 12%; Congo: 28%; Gabon: 1%; Equatorial Guinea: 37%; Central African Republic: 1% and Chad: 30%. Most of these FDI is absorbed by oil or mining operations.

The quality of a country's infrastructure, its governance and the quality of its human resources determine its attractiveness as an FDI destination. While the business environment is addressed first, the reputation of institutions and the extent of corruption make Cameroon a less privileged destination for FDI flows. However, the main constraint for the Central African region as a whole is the low level of development of financial markets, which hinders portfolio investment in particular. A good investment policy based on production site competitiveness levers that prioritizes horizontal actions aimed at optimizing projects to create potential (human resources, water, electricity, telephone, roads, railways, airports, ports, etc.) helps to attract FDI.

Capturing Sovereign Funds in the Form of FDI: States having surplus of national savings decide to make it profitable in investments abroad in the form of treasury bills, shares, bonds, and in the acquisition or construction of real estate. The capital from state resources is referred to as Sovereign Wealth Funds. Created in 1953, it has rapidly expanded since 2005 thanks to the activism of its holders who have made them a strategic instrument in the service of diplomacy. They are seeking opportunities, particularly in the infrastructure and construction sectors. From official sources, sovereign assets mobilized by some 30 countries are estimated at $3 billion in 2010. A tiny part of this capital is invested in the form of FDI.

Applying Environmental Taxation

Under the United Nations Framework Convention on Climate Change (UNFCCC), developed countries have committed to providing developing countries with additional financial resources to help them meet the costs of adapting to the adverse effects of climate change and provide the financial resources necessary for the transfer of environmentally sound technologies.

With regard to the volume of financing that can be mobilized, there are several estimates: the United Nations Department of Economic and Social Affairs estimates that USD 500 to 600 billion is needed annually by developing countries to support measures to combat climate change.

The British economist Nicholas Stern[50], estimated that the annual cost of the global fight against climate change represents 2% of global GDP, which was 1000 billion in 2006, and will rise to 2000 billion dollars in 2050. It was advocated that developed countries should provide $130 billion per year to developing countries through carbon trading.

For adaptation measures alone, the UNFCCC Secretariat has estimated the total annual costs at between $40 billion and $170 billion; the costs of protecting ecosystems amounting to $350 billion. The African group has estimated its financing needs at 5% of global GDP (USD 50 billion in 2006) to address climate change. Cameroon will get its part to support the competitiveness of its economy.

Making Mining and Petroleum Taxation a Factor for Adjusting Investment

The government has an alternative regulator of financial and social tensions through the adjustment of income from underground resources. Taxation and para-fiscal charges on minerals would provide the Government with an important part of the financing for its industrialization program. Flexible fuel prices at the pump could siphon off potentially harmful liquidity that carries inflationary risks.

---

[50] Report on the economics of climate change for the British government. *Stern Review Report on the Economics of Climate Change*, is a Review produced by a team led by N. Stern. In the October 2006 edition, he describes climate change as an economic externality. Stern subsequently addressed climate change as the greatest economic failure ever. The problem of climate change undermines market fundamentals: those that destroy by emitting greenhouse gases and generally do not pay, and others that suffer and pay.

Taking Advantage of Opportunity Offered by Crowd funding

Born like many other movements in the United States, Crowd funding connects a project leader seeking funding with a community of funders. Legislated by Barack OBAMA on 5 April 2012, crowd funding is deployed through a digital platform for charitable or return-on-investment projects, more particularly Start-ups, who find funds through an Internet community in the form of Equity Crowd funding, where the public becomes a shareholder of the company by acquiring shares in exchange for the funds invested. This creates a co-production relationship. Lending Crowd funding makes the public creditors of the company in return for repayment from the expected profits of the project. Crowd funding thus enables SMEs to:

- be free from the formalism of systemic banks;
- democratize shareholding;
- participate in the company's capital;
- painlessly and rapidly;
- address an extremely large audience through the web;
- Speed up the investment potential of any sector.

In the absence of sedimentation of good practices due to the youth of this mechanism, crowd funding is nevertheless emerging as a strong response for the revolution of industry and financial relations on a societal scale driven by the web. It is therefore incumbent on the Government to create an enabling environment and implement reforms in terms of financial sector liberalization and securing the legal framework. There is therefore a great need for institutional, legal and regulatory support to ensure that crowd funding modalities are appropriate.

Wealth creation in the 21st century could be leveraged by crowd funding, although it provides fragmented financing and/or in bits.

CONCLUSION

The problem to be tackled in order to bring Cameroon to the firmament of emerging countries will obviously remain the effectiveness of its leadership and management in the economic, financial, administrative and social spheres. To this end, the actors in the system must increase the pace of programs implementation of which obviously depends on a public procurement system that needs to be improved in terms of transparency and integrity. From this point of view, systematic mobilization of all actors is more than a wish to better manage the increasing sources of funding. Efforts should also be made to ensure that ODA provides a response.

CHAPTER VII:

EMERGENCE? YES, BUT... NOT BY 2035

"We can have nostalgia for great conquerors like Cyrus, Alexander the Great, Caesar, Genghis Khan, Isabella of Castile, Napoleon, and all those whom our history textbooks adulated as having led their people to glory. The current world leaders and citizens will have to do so with courage, mental energy and resolution, drawn from one's own intelligence and creativity, the means to overcome in a fight against the forces of the unknown whose immensity and destructive capacity we are only beginning to feel". Samuel PISAR: "Le Sang de L'Espoir (The Blood of Hope)"1979.

To criticize what is now recognized as biblical truth, namely the emergence by 2035, does not mean engaging in exaggerated nihilism or intellectual fantasy like Lewis Carroll' (1832-1898) in Alice in Wonderland[51]. It is simply a matter of finding a way out of the bad tracks that have prevented industrial Cameroon from seeing the light of day despite multiple attempts.

The truth is that emergence encompasses economic, social, technological and cultural content that is not reflected in the pedantic slogans that garnish political discourse. It is neither the end of a country's history nor its

---

[51] Lewis Carroll (1832-1898) is an English writer, mathematician and logician, who became very famous for his "Alice in Wonderland", published in 1865.

accession to the stage of developed economy. It is a movement that almost all developing countries have initiated, with different agendas, to reach the level of upper middle-income countries.

Emergence is even possible to be achieved by 2035, but the condition is that the country totally changes its industrial policy management software, putting in appropriate rhythms and rates, but above all, voluntarism. It will have to be based on the bold ambition to invest massively and qualitatively in the real locomotives of the Emergence train. History recognizes that over the past fifty years, the country's industrial dynamics have been linked to relative urban prosperity, fluctuating agricultural production due to bad weather, importation of industrial inputs and technical assistance for manufacturing and major construction sites. At the moment, things have fundamentally changed at the global level.

The knowledge economy, information and communication networks and flows, changes in consumption patterns, security and environmental threats are producing new local, national and global challenges every day which need to be addressed.

Table 36: The Performance of Cameroon on the Way of Emergence

TITLE	2016	2018
Global competitiveness Index	116th /137	121st /140
Institutions:	100th	125th
Infrastructures	129th	125th
ICT adoption	123rd	131st
Macroeconomic stability:	86th	76th
Health	114th	132nd
Skills	103rd	111th
Product market	114th	109th
Labour market	79th	106th
Financial system	97th	130th
Market size	83rd	89th
Business dynamism	111th	117th
Innovation capability	77th	109

Other relevant data in 2018:

Population (millions): 24.3; GDP per capita in US dollars: 1, 400; 10-year average annual GDP growth %: 4.1; GDP (PPP) % GDP: $89.54 billion (world 0.07); GDP - per capita: $ 3,700.

GDP - composition, by end use:_ Household consumption: 66.3%;_Government consumption: 11.8%; Investment in fixed capital: 21.6%; **GDP composition by sector of origin:_**Agriculture: 16.7%; Industry: 26.5%; Public: 56.8%; Unemployment rate %: 4.2; 5-year average; FDI inward flow % GDP: 2.1; Inclusive Development Index: 3.3 (1-7 best); Global Gender Gap Index: 0.7 (0-1 gender parity); Income Gini: 45.6 (0: perfect equality) to 100 (perfect inequality).

Table 37:Industrial and economic rating

YEARS	INDICATORS	SCORE	WORLD RANK OVER 191
2017	Industrial production growth rate:	3.3%	94
	Labour force	9.912 million	52
	COST ESTIMATES Revenues expenditures	5.363 billion 6.556 billion	
	Taxes and other revenues:	15.3% (of GDP)	
	Budget surplus (+) or deficit (-):	-3.4% (of GDP)	143
2017 2016	Public debt:	36.9% of GDP 32.5% of GDP	143
2017 2016	Inflation rate (consumer prices):	0.6 0.9	31
2017 2016	Current account balance:	-$932 million -$1.034 billion	141
2017 2016	Exports:	$4.732 billion $4.561 billion	111
2017 2016	Imports:	$4.812 billion $4.827 billion	
2017 2016	Reserves of foreign exchange and gold	$3.235 billion $2.26 billion	107

1. WHY EMERGENCE WOULD NOT TAKE PLACE BY 2035

Apart from the cities of Douala, Edea and Yaoundé, Kribi and Limbe to a certain extent, Cameroon's other cities are home to very few major industrial activities; hence the need to make expectations that could shape another future for Cameroon industry. This concern stems from a distressing observation that Cameroon's cities are growing in such a Kafkaesque disorder that it is difficult to give them a modern profile. The waste of economic and land resources in the current or emerging cities is just as absurd.

Clearly, the option taken by institutions in charge of urban policies is to act in a piecemeal fashion, rather than retreating in the face of social pressure. This has ended up putting the country in a kind of fatality characterized by the real or supposed impossibility of implementing urbanization master plans (where they exist). The political will to restructure cities is not the subject of permanent communication or compromise between governments, the private sector and citizen organizations. And, since decisions are made in a discretionary or authoritarian manner, they are not accepted by the populations concerned, but generate rejection or wrath.

For some analysts who find it impossible to urbanize the city of Yaoundé according to standards, the alternative would be the creation of a new political capital; which is far from being a Cameroonian invention. However, it is still possible to do things more methodically despite the political, financial, social and environmental cost of reformatting large cities. This can be done through courageous leadership, good strategies and smart planning, which free the country from the contradictions of a system inherited from colonization. Indeed, the occupation of urban space is still marked by the sociological proximity of migrants from tribes and agglutinated in the periphery, the creation of economic activities dipped in communities and a constant reference to customs. This form of dependent urbanization has been described by Milton Santos as "demographic urbanization" as opposed to “technological urbanization in developed countries. Sophie Bessis finds that there is no such thing as a "clear division between the city and the countryside. The frequent survival of agricultural and livestock activities in or around the city reflects this integration of the countryside into the city[52]".

The other striking fact of urban reality in Cameroon is the existence of a proliferation of non-competitive activities in an unbridled informal sector, alongside an atrophied modern sector.

The undocumented sector, which harbours small trades, sustains an ever-increasing mass of the population that has no access to modern, so-called decent jobs. Social and economic inequalities are blatant, as well as the most indescribable poverty that coexists with the insolent opulence of an opportunistic petty bourgeoisie made up of profiteers of the opacity of the public procurement system. Blocks of residential neighbourhoods are therefore inhabited by new wealthy people, a privileged class of mostly pushy people, who have acquired a fortune thanks to the parasitic positions occupied in the State apparatus.

2. CONDITIONS FOR AN EVENTUAL ACHIEVEMENT OF EMERGENCE BY 2035

Hypothesis

Consensus is emerging in the decision makers' sphere on the diversification of agricultural, industrial and mining sectors, as well as on the competitiveness of value chains.

The stakes of the harbour:

- Increasing the processing rate of agro-pastoral products while promoting inclusive development of all stakeholders through a vertically integrated approach;

[52] Sophie Bessis (1991): Op.cit.

- Uplifting the technological profiles of transformation by a better control of innovative transformation procedures and processes;
- Deepening the agro-industrial paths through a deeper horizontal diversification of the corresponding trades.

Strategic Actions:

Develop and operationalize structuring agro-industrial techno-poles over the national territory;

Strengthen the integration of agro-industrial sectors with other structuring industrial harbours (energy, digital), foundations (financing, infrastructure) and pillars (forest and wood); improve the competitiveness of food industries by strengthening and sustaining upgrading programmes.

Create New Comparative Advantages

Cameroon has assets to shorten its path to industrial emancipation.
All what should be done is that it's itinerary should be reviewed and strategic and operational approach innovated. There is no Table of the Law that serves as a reference in this area. The dynamics of industrialization are based on a process of Trial jumps and, since there is no free trial, the price must be paid, i.e. the appropriate means must be put in place to progress towards clearly defined objectives.

The markets targeted by the development of Construction and Civil Engineering are numerous; they range from the supply of aggregates for the construction of individual housing, to clusters of social housing, university campuses and cities, administrative buildings, buildings for commercial, cultural or strategic use, engineering structures and monuments. In total, billions in foreign currency will be spent and earned over time.

The factoring of sector-based assets which reconfigure the cross-referencing of identified inputs requires the use of new labour skills. The production of Construction and Civil Engineering products will be intensively ploughed, while financial capital will become a factor in accelerating building construction and consequently reducing construction site completion times.

This strategic shift may constitute a surprise as opinions, not the least of which, continue to fantasize about the agro-food sector on which vain hopes were once based. Socio-professional mobility, which is part of the genes of the Construction and civil engineering sector, is likely to disrupt economic and strategic relationships, and the ways in which natural, human, financial and logistical resources are organized and managed.

Emergence is not only associated with soaring GDP growth rates; it is also associated with the ability to transform natural assets to improve the environment and quality of life.

An Appropriate Framework for the Creation of Joint Ventures

The strategy for welcoming partners to the joint venture must be developed with a view to improving the business climate. The implementation of a major capital investment programme would provide a pool of employment and income opportunities; however, for national economic operators, critical size companies should be created to avoid specialization in marginal tasks of stone collectors, sand delivery workers or simple handlers, positions that would increase their vulnerability to cyclical hazards or technological change. Construction companies will have to integrate vertically upstream, with metallurgical or quarrying groups, and downstream, with producers of finishing and embellishment materials for buildings.

Horizontally, they will be able to develop agreements to conquer markets in the territory and in the sub-region. Three strategic challenges emerge here: (a) the optimization of production capacities, (b) flexible or polyvalent specialization and (c) the geographical mobility of companies.

Optimal capacity utilization and specialization are in line with the construction industry, which is a long-term business. The impact of sudden technological changes will be mitigated by capitalizing on the means of production and the consumption habits of the sector's goods, which are able to withstand the effects of fashion. Geographical mobility will also help to penetrate the regional or international market through direct investments in the form of relocation, alliance or joint venture operations.

Thus, increasing size, specialization and internationalization are strategies that Cameroonian construction companies can use to improve their internal and external competitiveness and protect themselves from economic, technological or social turbulence.

Reducing Sector Vulnerability

The Construction and Civil Engineering industry taken as an example is marked by the invasion of imported materials (more than 80%), which is a source of vulnerability and exposure to exogenous shocks. Thus, the good prospects for domestic demand are systematically siphoned off by extroversion created by the import of inputs, intermediate and/or finished products; hence the need to reverse trends by increasing production capacities in line with market and skills developments.

The lack of capacity is doubly damaging due to

(1) Domestic market shares upsurge likely to turn into a supply-side constraint and,

(2) Possible transformation of this weakness into a general factor of inflation if faced with potential demand increase.

This view is shared by Christian Penda EKOKA (1997): "The same extroversion is observed in the construction of roads, ports, bridges, buildings, airports, stadiums, etc. through the systematic recourse of companies, technologies and foreign financing, without any perception of a strategy to involve or develop local SMEs in the Civil Engineering sector[53]". And, he adds: "Apart from the wages of a low-skilled workforce and some career materials, other professional services related to construction (design, education) come from outside[54]".

Expanding Capacity, Optimizing Specialization and Geographical Mobility

The objective of increasing the size of firms must be to remain efficient and competitive on the market while at the same time making progress on the new opportunities offered by emerging materials. This expansion requires the upstream integration of metallurgical groups and, horizontally, partnerships with construction companies.

These partnerships aim at ensuring a specialization exuding economies of scale, improving division of labour and profitable value chains. FDI in the form of direct establishment, relocation of foreign firms, alliance or joint venture operations, external growth or acquisition of stakes in existing or future firms, will facilitate the strengthening of production capacities. The restructuring of material production companies is part of logic of appropriation of technologies and standards. The specialization of these

---

[53] Penda Ekoka, C. (1997): "Cameroon toward the 3rd Millennium)" ; EDI'ACTION, p.54.
[54] Ditto

units in each segment of the value chain would be sustainable if they could improve their bargaining power vis-à-vis their suppliers and customers.

The imbalance in foreign trade in the construction and civil engineering sector in Cameroon is an undeniable sign of the insufficient aggressiveness of national companies, not only to satisfy the domestic market but also to export. The high penetration rate of foreign companies and products and the erosion of competitive positions are signs of sector fragility.

Integrating Ecology into Industrial Competitiveness

The competitiveness of construction companies is over-determined by investment in innovation in the quality of materials. The main competitiveness indicators, such as creativity, productivity, return on capital, financial position and factor mix, reflect the strength or otherwise of the industry within an economy.

The consideration of ecological constraints in site selection and building design now influences R&D in alternative techniques and materials. The operation of companies in the sector and business-to-business (B-to-B) exchanges should promote an ecological culture aimed at a lower level of waste than the norm and facilitate the appropriation of clean processes and technologies. A global policy of anticipation in the face of new nature protection challenges will make it possible to effectively manage the risks of nuisance. However, environmental actions should not be seen simply as constraints, but also as opportunities that companies should seize in their marketing approach and as a competitive strategy.

Systematizing the Use of Standards & Labels to be Competitive

Laws and regulations will not be enough to improve the business climate. The encouragement of good practices, education in good morals and the appropriation of the instruments developed within the framework of Soft Law are assets for good business governance. The central idea is that companies and administrations should make a commitment to avoid behaviour that negatively affects their reputation. The aim is not to promote a phenomenon of religious fundamentalism, otherworldliness or puritanism, but to provide a response to a societal project capable of improving governance at all levels, based on incentives and on the individual and collective will for change. Christine DRULLION believes that reputation is an essential element of the strategy of large companies for: « 94% of American bosses; 86% French bosses, and 71% German bosses".

The systematic use of ISO standards would serve to foster consensus on good managerial practices based on product quality and customer satisfaction, such as ISO 9001:2008, which provides a set of standard requirements for a quality management system, regardless of the scope and size of the user organization. It makes it possible to adopt a systemic approach to managing production processes that stimulates the ortho-functioning of an organization, as a tool that generates trust between customers and suppliers. ISO 14001 certification allows a company to have its policy and processes certified as compliant with the constraints relating to the development, implementation, maintenance and evaluation of an environmental management system. The generalization of compliance with standards, codes of ethics and professional conduct aims to win the war against laxity, flaws, fraud and corruption without firing a single shot.

Significantly Improving the Quality of Governance

With regard to governance, Cameroon's reputation is globally established in terms of conflict management of electoral processes, obstructions to individual and collective freedoms, the narrowing of the citizen space due to terrorism laws, slow promotion of gender equality, embezzlement of public funds, collusion and influence peddling. The diagnosis of the National Institute of Statistics (NIS), a state agency, is not tender on this subject: "Lack of governance, the cost of corruption, weak institutions constrain business and slow economic growth. Taxation, unequal access to credit, and relations with administrations are major constraints to business development[55]".

For Thomas WOLF and EMINE GÜRGEN, "corruption at the highest level must be minimized, as it hinders growth and has a corrosive effect on society in general, since it is basically the highest authorities who are the moral guide of the rest of society[56]". And the NIS to specify: "A poor business environment is a brake on the competitiveness of companies and a brake on the attractiveness of the FDI that Cameroon needs[57]".

Table 38: Assessment (in percentage) of governance by type of companies

Type of companies	Good	Fairly good	Bad	No opinion	ND	Total
VSE	4.0	19.9	57.5	10.5	8.1	100.0
SE	4.4	20.2	55.2	10.3	10.0	100.0
ME	2.9	23.5	52.2	10.9	10.3	100.0
LE	4.3	31.1	42.6	12.5	9.6	100.0
Total	4.4	22.8	52.4	10.8	8.5	100/0

Source: NIS/GEC 2009

55 General Enterprises Census, Thematic Report; 2009; p. 89.
56 Thomas Wolf and Emine Gürgen (July 2004): Governance and anti-corruption in the Baltic States and CIS countries: the role of the IMF.
57 General Enterprises Census, Thematic Report; 2009; p. 8.

This table shows that there is less than 4.4% of good opinion, against 52.4% of bad judgment on the governance of all companies. “The obstacles most frequently cited by entrepreneurs are, in order of importance, taxation: 58.8%; corruption: 50.6%; access to credit: 37.6%; administrative formalities: 35.2%; unfair competition: 25.8%; infrastructure: 18.4% and, the cost of credit: 18%[58]”.

Table 39: Main obstacles to competitiveness by sub-sector

Obstacles	Extraction	Food industries	Other industries Manufacturing	Electricity, water, gas	Construction
Taxation	61.5	74	66.2	50	66.4
Corruption	46.2	63	57.3	47.6	61.6
Access denied	46.2	37.6	42.9	45.2	56.8
Administrative procedures	30.8	38.7	37.9	35.7	38.4

Source: NIS/GEC 2009

In 2010, the World Bank's Doing Business Report, the World Economic Forum's World Competitiveness Index, Transparency International's Corruption Perceptions Index, the UNDP Human Development Report, the Bertelsmann Foundation's Transformation Index on Societal Changes in Developing Countries in Favour of Democracy and the Market Economy, all agree on Cameroon's weak progress in governance. And yet, the country was well ranked on the main Pillars of Competitiveness of the WEF: macroeconomic stability (15th / 133); public debt (16th / 133). But the signals are reversed when it comes to the Institutions and Diversion of Funds pillar, where only four countries are worse than Cameroon ranked 129th out of 133.

[58] National Institute of Statistics / General Enterprises Census 2009.

Paradoxically, the official reaction to the publication of the rankings deemed disappointing suggests a plot against the Republic.

In any case, the rankings are not a conspiracy or a relentless act either, since the exercise affects almost all the countries of the world annually. The best thing for low-rated countries is to make efforts to improve their ranking, which influences market access and raises the cost of borrowing capital.

Rebuilding Corporate Governance on Micro-Cultures

In Cameroon, adapting management methods to local micro-cultures is a serious matter. Georges GALLAIS-HAMMONO discovers for Africa, a management broken down into four cultural dimensions:

- "A paternalistic authority of a feudal type;
- Weak control of uncertainty, resulting in a certain fatalism;
- A community spirit that takes precedence over individualism, the company being lived as a village;
- A female culture that favours social over material, prefers a good working atmosphere and salary security over creativity[59]".

Marc PENOUIL believes that: "the African enterprise is a place of power before being a place of combination of factors[60]", while ETOUNGA MANGUELE ironically invokes a necessary Cultural Adjustment.

[59] Gallais-Hammono G. Professor at the University of Orléans, Director of the Orléans Institute of Finance in: "Public Enterprises and Development: An African panorama".

[60] Marc PENOUIL is Professor of Economics, Chairperson of the University of Bordeaux I: "The Future of African Enterprise" in,

3. CORPORATE SOCIAL RESPONSIBILITY (CSR) AND SOCIALLY RESPONSIBLE INVESTMENT (SRI) AS THE CORNERSTONE OF COMPETITIVENESS

In Cameroon, the twin concepts of Corporate Social Responsibility (CSR) and Socially Responsible Investment (SRI) are reserved for public eloquence for a class of civil servants, experts, consultants, academics and civil society. The companies whose creation is so encouraged are protected for the tax revenues they provide and the jobs they generate. Notably, companies in the strategic sector benefit from some protection and take advantage of the tolerance if not complicity of State powers to avoid their social and environmental responsibilities.

As a result, CSR is no longer a strategic choice, but "an imperative inherent to the nature of the new millennium enterprise, illustrated by the emerging concept of the Citizen Enterprise" (Champion, 2003). Bruno REBELLE, former Director of International Campaigns at Greenpeace: “we agree that companies exist to make a profit, but they must be aware of the consequences of the way they do it[61]”. CSR therefore proposes to introduce the influence of increasingly informed, demanding and militant consumers between the invisible hand of the market and the visible hand of the State.

For Logsdon and Yuthas (1997), “does the strategic problem statement of this concept confirm the company in its traditional role of maximizing profit, while moral concern statement raises the issue of social responsibility as an educational challenge aimed at making a company a

---

Mélanges en l'honneur de Jean -Guy MERIGOT, under the supervision of André LABOURDETTE. ECONOMICA.

[61] Bruno Rebelle, former Director of the international NGO Greenpeace and Advisor on Policy and Development Strategy.

subject whose moral capacities must be uplifted?" However, in a context of chronic corruption, companies are on the waves of institutional complicities to carry out activities that disrespect human rights, disregard societal impacts and are unaccountable in the name of competitiveness.

Jérôme Frantz's (2010) recommendations encourage the creation of a sustainable competitive advantage based on the implementation of CSR: - maintain a database of organizations with norms, standards and labels; - receive from the State exemplary practice of CSR and the benefits of governance within the framework of financing policies with social and societal clauses; - create a Ministry and Observatories of CSR; - promote the rapprochement of companies in the territory by participating in projects with a strong mutual impact.

Despite their broad approval, CSR and SRI have their opponents; among the most virulent, the Nobel Prize winner for economics, the American Milton Friedman of the neoclassical trend who, in the 1960s, declared: "Few developments could undermine the very foundations of our free society as deeply as the acceptance by leaders of a social responsibility other than to make as much money as possible for their shareholders. It is a fundamentally subversive doctrine[62]".

This position is part of a program at Warwick University in Great Britain; it teaches that morality and business do not work together; that corruption and bribery are considered normal and acceptable in various parts of the world and that they are necessary to build a business network with politicians.

---

[62] Friedman, Milton: Capitalism and Freedom, 1962.

From the point of view of Business Ethics, these positions of a monetarist and a few isolated researchers are also considered as subversion. They have not prevented CSR and its twin, SRI, from gaining notoriety and becoming a theoretical corpus taught in several universities around the world. They are referenced as a marketing tool, particularly by multinational companies threatened by militant pressure from civil society activists or anti-globalization activists. It is therefore a legitimate theme on a global scale, more particularly since the Earth Summit in Rio de Janeiro in 1992 and the adoption by 150 countries of Agenda 21, the first of 27 principles of which is: "Human beings are at the heart of sustainable development concerns. They have the right to a healthy and productive life in harmony with nature". The globally shared objective being:

"Economically viable, environmentally sustainable, and socially equitable development", a synthesis of the three pillars of sustainable development based on the triple P: People, Planet, Profit (or Prosperity), which links macroeconomic concern for GDP growth with human and ecological management. The socialized enterprise becomes a laboratory of democracy for shareholders, organized citizens and managers, to pose and solve societal problems and repair industrial damage on nature, the society and people.

4. URGENCY MEASURES TO IMPROVE COMPETITIVENESS FOR EMERGENCE

Cameroon is experiencing real difficulties in connecting to the global economy because of the languor of its bureaucracy and its traditions, which have become prohibitive in terms of economic expansion and social progress.

Economic integration within the Central African Sub-region, one of the slowest of all the Regional Economic Communities (RECs) in the world, is an inhibiting factor in industrial competitiveness. The level of intra-zone trade is desperately low (1% of the total), social indicators are at their lowest with a quasi-stationary HDI of about 0.418; 45% average of the population living on less than a dollar a day; 20 to 35% unemployment rate and more than 70% underemployment.

Even more, less than 5% of the water in the Congo Basin is used for irrigated agriculture, and only 2 to 12% of arable land is used for a 25% contribution to GDP; the food deficit is made up by a massive import of food from the continent.

Table 40: Progress of the integration process in Central Africa

EXPORTS	2.000	2,001	2,002	2,003	2,004	2,005	2,006
Into ECCAS	87.5	95.8	81.7	115.7	93.3	76.0	100.4
Total Exports	1,083.5	1,099.3	1,062. 3	1,104.1	1,059.4	1,318.9	1,620.1
ECCAS ratio/Total	8%	8.7%	7.7%	10.5%	8.8%	5.8%	6.2%
IMPORTS							
From ECCAS	22.8	35	19.2	13.9	28.4	47	106.2
Total Imports	365.4	400.8	350.9	370.2	398.3	657.9	731.5
ECCAS ratio/Total	6.2%	8.7%	5.5%	3.7%	7.1%	7.1%	14.5%

Source: UNECA/BSR. Flyer 2009

From 2000 to 2006, Cameroon exported goods for an annual average of CFAF 1,193 billion (about USD 2.4 billion), including 93 billion (about USD 0.19 billion) to the ECCAS zone, or 7.8%. With regard to imports over the same period, 39 billion CFA francs of goods came from ECCAS out of a total of 468 billion CFA francs; i.e. a ratio of 8.3%. In general, the goods traded, were heavy, perishable food products with low trade margins.

A systemic neutralization of the economies of the Sub-region we are as witnessed at the industrial level, with each Community member producing identical or substitutable manufactured goods, so as not to depend on the other. However, Cameroon, despite being a neighbour of a country like Nigeria with a population of more than 170 million, lacked an offensive strategy to penetrate this market, if only through niches, to offset its massive imports of capital goods, particularly spare car parts and other manufactured products, from this giant neighbour.

Cameroon thus was lagging far behind in adapting to the pace of technological change; and was developing a low resilience to contra-cyclical economic, food, energy and financial crises.

In addition, because of the double effect of poorly executed work and the lack of maintenance of acquired fixed capital, the poor sustainability of infrastructure caused the government to lose money while making corrupt players in the investment chain happy. As honey catches more flies than vinegar, the ongoing or projected exploitation of mining deposits will still make Cameroon a field of geopolitical rivalry between the major powers through multinational corporations.

5. ADAPTING QUALITY OF ENTREPRENEURS IN RELATION TO NUMBER OF COMPANIES

In the euphoria of the celebration of company registrations, the unemployed are eagerly awaiting the publication of job offers, and observers want to see those of the Start Up who are coming out of it as soon as possible. In this baby boom of companies, the first judgments will also focus on the growth differential in their Early Stage. But the problem is much less that of companies than that of entrepreneurs.

Jacques GIROIRE, President of the Association Progrès du Management (APM), a division of the Conseil National du Patronat Français (CNPF), said: “Business leaders receive little training.” They always have an excuse, whereas we need competitive, ambitious, determined leaders. Our idea is to take the best from those who want to question themselves. On the one hand, there is research-experimentation that calls on advisors; intelligence and future scenarios for which we call on visionaries, gurus of sorts. It is therefore up to each promoter to write its own history, to invent a unique industrial trajectory. From there, knights were born in this noble and risky profession of entrepreneurship. However, cultural, casting, coaching, mentoring and consulting are called upon in the arbitration of this encounter.

Marc PENOUIL pointed out that "modern companies created in the African context are finding it increasingly difficult to operate in a normal way because of the absence of real entrepreneurs. The transition to modern business structures, in a cultural context which was not always ready to welcome it, seems to be one of the main causes of the failures recorded.

The difficult transition of Cameroon economy could also be explained by the fact that more than 90% of the entrepreneurial landscape in the mid-2010s is in the undocumented sector, and that viable companies in the formal sector are either joint ventures or the majority of which are foreign capital owned.

Within the landscape of informal activities, Marc PENOUIL distinguishes two categories: those that can evolve towards the structured sector and others, which will not be able to do so even in the long term because of their involute nature. He succeeded in extracting 7 main groups from the non-modern sector activities; the first four are likely to involution and the last three to evolutionary transformation:

- a part of the traditional craft industry;
- survival activities;
- development sub-trades, creators of a monetized economic circuit;
- the parallel economy, which operates at the border of legality, but brings in big profits;
- the informal, structured financial sector, which is highly branched by infra-social links;
- African association trust funds and various community self-help associations;
- Pre-modern activities: producing at lower prices than the modern sector.

The shift from these activities to the formal sector depends, according to Mr PENOUIL, on the conditions likely to encourage entrepreneurs to modernize their operations, in particular, the transformation of the economic and social environment thanks to the eclecticism of political choices and the leadership of leaders, who favour the adaptation of financing tools, the quality of training for the appropriation of technological changes, the raising of the infrastructure standard.

ETOUNGA MANGUELE[63], in asking himself whether it would be necessary to make a cultural adjustment, Alain HENRY answers: "Even if the difficulties of companies remain numerous, particularly in the political or economic sphere, it is possible to effectively improve their management. However, an effort should be made to take a

[63] D. Etounga Manguelle (1991): “Does Africa need a Cultural Adjustment Program?”. Ed. Nouvelles du Sud, Paris.

closer look at local realities[64]". And, he concludes: "Finally, with regard to SMEs that are still part of the Terra Incognita, it is necessary to seek a better understanding of the social and economic logic to which they are subject. The time for this reflection should seem very light compared to the years of maturation to come.

Obviously, it is not only maturing that would take years; there is also the inevitable work of repairing the mistakes made, the impacts of which are inevitably irreversible. In both cases, a choice of civilization should be made that goes beyond mere speculation on productive models. Because it is men who make civilization! Hence our temptation to embrace Olivier PASSET's project to create an industrial strike force.

6. CREATE A TASK FORCE FOR COMPETITIVE INDUSTRY IN CAMEROON

The criteria that Cameroon should display in its attempt to rise to the pinnacle of the New Industrial Countries are essentially twofold:

- Diversify its industrial production and competitive exports, and,
- Triple or even quadruple its per capita income in twenty years.

However, the country's economic performance indicates a low internal and external competitiveness of national companies, a low-aggressive trade policy and a structural inability to organize the assault on markets considered buoyant. Arguably, low competitiveness in Cameroon goes hand in hand with low labour and capital productivity,

---

[64] Alain Henry: *Companies in Africa: Little-known progress*; article published by AFRICA 2000 in its third quarter 1993 issue.

which means that overall and per capita income is poorly redistributed.

The challenge facing the country thus comes from the low capacity of its companies to have the Industrial Task Force. From this instrumental softness, strategic choices in the field of industrial action are comparable to those made by the military headquarters; the usual reference to captains of industry to designate competent managers who lead firms and succeed in obtaining results is not neutral.

Staff work is carried out in secret and involves only a small group of smart, bold and far-sighted experts who prepare strikes that can create serious impacts. Some industry strategists have a flair for selecting profitable targets and anticipating the profitability of certain niches. Then, they structure logistical, human and financial resources to invest massively and qualitatively in businesses with high return potential.

The timing of hitting the identified targets depends on the risk calculation. These strike forces may be based on a diversity of activities whose profitability is considered very high or, thanks to innovation, rehabilitate declining branches or sectors. The industrial strike force thus depends on the quality of human resources that predetermines the accuracy of the attack, the expectation of a significant gain as well as the impact of the firms involved on the economy and society.

It is also necessary to declare a state of industrial emergency as a strategy for the general mobilization of intelligence, productive forces, knowledge and know-how, with a fixed or flexible agenda.

7. NEW ECONOMIC GEOGRAPHY (NEG) AND CHALLENGE OF COMPETITIVENESS.

Geo-economics began to be theorized in the 1990s. It was based on the attractiveness of a territory within the framework of industrial analysis (Baldwin et al. 2003), and attempted the following explanation: "The location of activities is only partially dependent on the initial factors endowment; it is also conditioned by agglomeration effects[65]".

Krugman (1991) and the proponents of this theory place the location of industries in the idea that location choices result from two types of antagonistic forces:

(a) Agglomeration forces that encourage companies to concentrate geographically in order to benefit from economies of scale and external economies. Among those, the existence of an area with a high purchasing power (outlet effect) is an important factor;

(b) Dispersal forces, which promote the spread of activities given the constraints of availability of natural resources and the fixed nature of certain factors of production[66]".

The NEG recognizes natural factor endowments and the cost of their implementation are one thing; but another thing is to develop non-factorial attractiveness, excluding costs, to make an entire country attractive to capital flows. This

---

[65] Krugman, quoted by Theophile DZAKA-KIKOUTA (2006), e-mail: dzaka_kikouta@yahoo.fr; CREP/INICA and Xavier BITEMO-NDIWULU E-mail: bitemox@yahoo.fr; 7th scientific days of the AUF Economic Analysis and Development Network on the theme of institutions and development (Paris, 6-7 September 2006).

[66] Krugman (1991): "The impact of the economic role of the State on the attractiveness of the territory of developing countries: the case of the mining and oil-producing countries of Central Africa[66]

influx may be aimed at concentrating on selected sectors or spreading throughout the entire productive fabric. The coherence of the public-private partnership in terms of the overall or sector-based competitiveness of the economy must be an objective to be achieved. Similarly, the rationality of R&D investments, coupled with strategic and organizational intelligence, will enable the success of this other policy.

8. NEW FORMS OF INVESTMENT FOR EMERGENCE

The transfer of technology that marked the economic literature of development in the aftermath of the independence of African countries is presently at the heart of the globalized labour market. Emphasis is laid on competitiveness, training, creativity, innovation and productivity, which are enriched by cultural diversity and alternative financial mechanisms. The “new forms of investment” that have emerged have contributed to the emergence of NICs (New Industrial Countries).

Table 41: Proportion(%) of industrial enterprises adopting innovative techniques by types of enterprise in Cameroon

Types of business	Use of research centre results	Research & experimental development	Acquisition of services from r & d	Machines equipment related to techno innovations.	Software external techno. external techno. innovations	Introduction of techno innovate. into market.	Training directly related to techno innovations.	other technological innovations
VSE	11	2.6	4	9.9	7.9	3.9	6.6	0.7
SE	7.8	3	1.2	7.9	6.1	1.8	4.2	1.2
ME	20	4.8	2.1	10.6	8.5	1.6	8.5	0.5
LE	18.2	11.1	1.9	13	13	3.7	14.8	1.9
Sub-sector								
Extracting	33.3	44.4	22.2	33.3	33.3	22.2	33.3	11.1
Food industry	14.8	2.5	0	4.2	1.8	1.7	5	0.8
Manufacturing Industry	10.2	2.9	2	11.8	9.4	2.8	8.2	1.2
Water and gas	28.6	14.3	9.5	19	14.3	4.7	14.3	0
Construction	15.7	4.2	2.4	8.5	8.5	1.2	5.5	0
Total	13.8	4.3	2.3	9.8	8.0	2.5	7.3	0.89

Source: NIS/GEC 2009

Table 42: Proportion(%) of industrial enterprises adopting innovative technologies by promoter/manager highest diploma

Highest diploma	Use of research centre results	Research & experimental development	Acquisition of r & d services	Machinery equipment related to technological innovations	External technician software related to tech innovation	Introduction of technological innovations into the market	Training directly related to technological innovations	Other technological innovations
Missing	15	2.5	3.8	7.6	6.3	5.1	8.9	1.3
without diploma	13.8	6.9	3.5	13.8	6.9	3.4	10.3	0
cep/fslc	19.2	3.9	0	0	0	0	0	0
bepc/cap/gceo	8.5	0	0	6.4	2.1	0	0	0
probatoire	0	7.1	0	0	7.1	0	0	0
bac/gce	5.8	1.4	1.4	5.4	2.7	1.4	1.4	1.4
bts/deug/nhd	17	3.9	3.9	13.5	11.5	5.8	7.7	1.9
Bachelor	19.6	5.4	1.8	17.7	14.3	3.6	5.4	0
master 1	17	6.9	3.4	10.2	5.1	1.7	6.8	1.7
dea/master +	15	6.4	2.4	12	13.6	1.6	15.2	0.8
total	13.8	4.3	2.3	9.8	8	2.5	7.3	0.9

Source: NIS/GEC 2009

Competition has gone beyond the exploitation of natural advantages and the use of abundant factors; it is now concerned with new products resulting from research and innovation efforts. The challenge remains the optimization of appropriation and yield of patents and licenses for a better production in volume and quality.

9. TECHNOLOGY TRANSFER TO IMPROVE COMPETITIVENESS

To be competitive, to innovate or produce technology goods, it is necessary to structure research and mobilize the necessary financing for its development. Daniel SOULIÉ and Dominique ROUX (1992) believe that "R & D expenditures lead to the emergence of knowledge, which is a capital for the company". For Guillaume THIBAULT (2008), "Industrial policy and innovation policy are inseparable in a globalized world[67]"; he proposes that competitiveness in industry should be re-established as a national cause, public and private research streamline, industrial policies redeployed towards SMEs, companies supported in a targeted manner, sources of financing diversified, promotion of company territorial anchoring carried out[68].

In Cameroon, if the University has not become a Centre of Excellence in the American-style, or a hotbed of ideas, neither has the company become a place of exaltation of competitiveness, productivity or creativity through proxy technologies. So, how could the company become competitive if it does not finance research programs on its own or in partnership with the State, local authorities and universities? And how can this be done if the University and

---

67 Guillaume Thibault (2008): "Industrial Strategy for France with regard to Globalization)", Editions Technip, page 276.

68 Op cit.

research centres are emptied of the holders of science? Raj Reddy: "What constitutes the wealth of a nation is the level of wisdom, knowledge, skills, ability to master new technologies for new jobs, and control of its own destiny; true power is the power of knowledge[69]".

10. DIGITAL GOVERNANCE TO SUPPORT INDUSTRIAL COMPETITIVENESS

Information Technology (IT) is now a force and driver of modern technological development and globalization, and is generally accepted as a key enabler of economic and technological growth. IT adoption has shown to propel the economies of nations to greater productivity and creates jobs. Information Technology has such great potential to improve business operations, education, technology and economic growth. This technology could help contribute to poverty alleviation in developing economies if used to meet local and national needs. There is an unequal access to Information and communication technology between developed and developing nations (Macharia & Gituru, 2006).

There is now a global increase in Internet penetration due to government led initiatives and private efforts (Andrade & Urquhart, 2009). In developed countries, IT has been used to create strategic advantage in business and various operations (Apulu & Lathan, 2009). Information Technology (IT) plays a vital role in leveraging productivity and efficiency in private organizations, governments and research (Al-Gahtani, 2003). Remarkable results from the application of IT in education, health, agriculture, and technology in developed nations show that such positive results can be replicated in African countries.

[69] Raj Reddy, of Carnegie Mellon University, cited by Samuel Pisar, in Human Resources.

The value of IT in any organization depends on its infrastructure. IT infrastructure is a set of shared tangible and intangible resources composed of computers, network and telecommunication technologies, data and core software applications (Duncan, 1996). Flexible IT infrastructure is vital in developing sustained competitive advantage, (Byrd & Douglas, 2001), and is a source of business value, (Fink & Neumann, 2009).

11. THE SOURCE OF EFFECTIVENESS IN INFORMATION TECHNOLOGY

Governments are to provide strategic policy framework for the acquisition and use of IT for social and economic growth. The development of IT infrastructures in emerging economies has been lagging behind those in developed countries because of poor policies and insufficient investments in the IT sector, (Laryea, 1999). Most developing countries (the case of Cameroon) have ineffective information technology policies and this has created problems in the growth and application of Information Technology. Governments of these countries acknowledge the need and importance of IT, but little concrete action has been taken in this area, (Enakrire & Onyenania, 2007).

Most developing countries do not have the resource to develop Information Technology in their respective countries. Rather, they depend on substantial foreign aid to ensure the development of Information Technology. Developed countries have also not done much to assist emerging nations to develop their information technology infrastructure, (Laryea, 1999). Nwaka, (2005), noted that funding from developed countries has been ineffective because they try to find local problems to suit pre-package assumptions and solutions, and do not incorporate local expertise in the process of solving the problems. Akubue, (2002), stated that many developing countries import technologies and its innovations without modification to suit their environment and culture.

In 1996, member states of the African Information Society Initiative (AISI) adopted an objective of creating an African Information Infrastructure through access to a global information infrastructure for development needs and to build their own National Information and Communication infrastructures. This has met with limited success. The Nigeria Information Technology Developing Agency (NITDA) developed a national IT policy to make Nigeria a key leading player in the information and computer technology by the year 2005. Some of the objectives of the policy include developing IT infrastructure, integrating IT into the mainstream of education and training, empowering Nigerians with effective IT skills and preparing them for global competitiveness. These objectives have not been fully met. In stressing the importance of effective national policy and adequate IT training Aniebonam (2005), called for a Nigerian Civil Service Enhancement with particular reference to IT capacity which will increase productivity and make Nigeria digitally competitive.

Information Technology infrastructure consists of computers, software and all components of telecommunication systems necessary to facilitate efficient data transfer and management (Enakrire & Onyenania, 2007). It also includes IT experts to design, install, maintain and fix systems, and skilled IT personnel to operate the system efficiently (Laryea, 1999). Poor Basic Information Technology infrastructure is the major cause of stagnation to the development of Information Technology in African and other developing countries (Omekwu, 2003). The essential infrastructure and networks to facilitate IT transfer, implementation and development is lacking in developing countries. This has made the accessibility to affordable telecommunication, computer and Internet difficult (NEPAD, 2003). Basic national IT infrastructure which is accessible to the people and connected to the world is of utmost importance in any country, and should be effectively integrated into the socio-economic and business life of the country. These IT resources are still scarce in many developing countries including access to hardware and software. Omekwu, 2003 noted that inadequate telecommunication infrastructure poses a major hindrance to IT adoption in developing countries.

Cameroon has a programme on e-governance. E-governance implies implementing government's logic in multiple parts of digital transformation projects and major projects between public institutions, the private sector and civil society; it is therefore a "mechanism" that combines politics, technical tools, animation methodologies and communication strategies. The impact of digitization on knowledge transfer justifies the introduction of the concept of the digital economy. The extraordinary growth in the supply and demand for physical infrastructure goods and services is an important driver of growth in countries where the ICT industry is located.

The factors that influence the take-off of ICTs and access to the digital economy can be grouped into four categories[70]:

- Physical network: Infrastructure, information and communication system;

---

[70] Fariselli, Patrizia (2007): Electronic Commerce for Development: General Framework. An article published in Electronic Commerce and Development, published by OECD Development Centre Studies, under the coordination of Andrea Goldstein and David O' Connor.

- Economic network: Industry (Markets and companies);
- Resources : Informational, human and financial;
- Politics: Global and sector-based strategies, legal and regulatory framework.

The way and intensity with which these factors are combined contribute to the widening or narrowing of the digital device. The priority is therefore to build new infrastructure and improve high-level training to achieve the critical mass of skills for the development of the sector's future competitiveness. The aim is to invest strategically in the ICT value chain and to adapt incentives to the industrialization of content in this field with high wealth creation potential.

Admittedly, Cameroon has not yet developed the capacity to engage in the highly oligopolistic semiconductor industry; but it can position itself in an industrial model of software development and content industrialization, as do many emerging or developing countries.

The specificity of the industrialization model of this sector can be found in:

- The generation, processing and transmission of information;
- Human resources from several knowledge areas:
- Creativity based on products and standards, which generates business ideas and guides other industrial players;
- The regional environment as the basis for a relevant market to produce and commercialise its products and services;

- The tendency of companies in the sector to integrate vertically and benefit from the complementarity of segments and the effect of synergies.

The exploitation of one-to-many e-commerce solutions, and services linked to marketing and information sites, which are real sources of opportunities, are still in their infancy in Cameroon, as e-business is not yet able to take off to stimulate commercial development despite the importance of public procurement in GDP.

Alignment with Community (Central Africa) directives should provide the telecom/ICT sector with the competitiveness capacities necessary for the State's integration into the world economy; in any case, the telecom/ICT sector is slowly evolving in Cameroon and the applications that emerge every day are not sufficiently developed. However, this sector is in a position to improve competitiveness for good industrial governance; an industry now focused on knowledge-intensive products and services.

Fabrice HERVIEU WANÉ and Bernard CASSEN affirm that "ICT structures the ways of learning, thinking, producing, exchanging, deciding and representing the world. Public authorities will therefore have to make their social appropriation one of the foundations of the education of the whole population[71]".

Sources from the General Business Census conducted in 2009 in Cameroon (INS/RGE 2009), out of 8035 companies selected in the primary, secondary and tertiary sectors,

- 78.3% of companies have a computer;
- 86.0% of employees know how to use a computer:

---

[71] Le Monde Diplomatique (Manière de voir N°41 de septembre-octobre 1998)

- 48.9% of these companies are connected to the Internet;
- 24.1% of companies have an intranet network; and
- 33.9% use the Internet for business operations (B2B).

Of course, these ratios could have been lower if they were calculated on the basis of the 11,685 industrial companies surveyed in 2009.

With a Digital Access Index of 0.16 (16%) in 2010, Cameroon, ranked 147th/178 countries, remains a digitally landlocked country. The ambition stated in the GESP is to raise this indicator to 0.47 by 2020; another challenge that will not be met.

These data sufficiently demonstrate the immense need for investment in infrastructure, network, equipment, operations, training, content industrialization, service provision and externalities management. The Telecom/ICT sector would thus become the engine of growth and competitiveness in Cameroon.

There are many opportunities in creation, innovation, segmentation, specialization in the range of old or new trades depending on the mesh of activity and demand in each niche; the aim is therefore to make decision-makers aware of the need to take transformative measures so that the backlog that is accumulating does not make it impossible to catch up, which would be very costly for all stakeholders. Cameroon should therefore learn "from India, China, South Korea, the diffusion of ICTs in regulation and targeted enforcement" (Benjamin Neumann, 2011).

Table 43: Proportion (%) of industrial enterprises using ICT and by type of enterprise

TYPES OF ENTERPRISES	Number of enterprises	Computer access rate (%)	Employees who know how to use a computer (%)	Internet connection (%)	Companies with an intranet network (%)	Companies using the internet for business operations (%)
VSE	293	84	89	53	25	46
SE	253	75	85	53	15	38
ME	296	89	96	76	38	64
LE	80	100	100	95	78	76
Sub-sector						
Extracting	16	100	100	78	67	78
Food industries	177	63	74	36	20	28
Manufacturing industries	412	88	93	74	36	60
Electricity, water and gas	31	96	100	74	43	70
Construction	286	93	99	70	29	56
Total	922	84	91	65	31	53

Source: NIS/GEC 2009

Table 44: Proportion (%) of sub-sectors of activity using ICT

SUB-SECTORS OF ACTIVITY	Number Of Companies	Access To The Computer (%)	Employees Who Know How To Use A Computer	Internet Connection	Companies With An Intranet Network	Companies Using The Internet For Business Operations
Agriculture	47	84.8	85.7	51.5	75.8	42.4
Livestock farming	8	42.9	57.1	42.9	0.0	28.6
Sylviculture	22	88.2	100.0	76.5	58.8	41.2
Fishing and fish farming	2	100.0	100.0	100.0	100.0	100.0
Sub-sector						
Extracting	14	100.0	100.0	77.8	66.7	77.8
Food industries	191	64.5	76.3	35.8	21.2	29.8
Other manufacturing industries	392	88.8	93.8	72.4	37.1	58.0
Electricity, water and gas	48	90.3	96.8	64.5	38.7	54.8
Construction	224	92.0	97.7	69.5	29.3	56.0
Trade	2,806	65.9	76.9	39.0	18.1	29.9
Transport	286	88.2	90.8	71.9	39.5	51.3
Bank and insurance	530	94.6	96.7	70.1	47.6	44.8
Other tertiary	3,340	81.8	88.7	45.9	19. 8	28.1
Total	8,035	78.3	86.0	48.9	24.1	33.9

Source: NIS/GEC 2009

A technological leap framed by a relevant digital economy and governance model would give greater perspective and success to strategic, instrumental or operational initiatives in this rapidly changing sector, whose effects and impacts on industrial activity and social transformation are often unpredictable.

12. COMMUNICATING AND REPORTING: EVERYTHING DEPENDS ON IT!

It would be an unfinished symphony to complete this essay without mentioning the thorny problem of communication and dissemination of data. The compilation of raw information in public or private organisations is often a source of irritation to those holding it, even if it is devoid of any strategic character. It may suddenly become a "**top-secret defence**" or **"medical confidentiality**" matter, and its sharing subject to hypothetical hierarchical authorisations.

Fundamentally, this sentimental protection of information is not always a matter of ill will; there is also incompetence (this is not an insult), as many public officials, including senior officials, handle data that is irrelevant, incomplete or disorganised and therefore not susceptible to transfer to an external analyst. Often, too, this refusal can pave the way for transactions that can lead to corrupt acts. Information then becomes a commodity to be sold under the table! Charles JEPSON, quoted by Alvin TOFLER, finds that: *"Information is the indispensable catalyst for change at all levels, and that is why its power is so formidable*[72]**"**. S. Pisar (1983) prophetically declared it: "*It has become impossible in a country to have an*

---

[72] Alvin Tofler (1990): Knowledge, Wealth and Violence and the Edge of the 21st Century, Bantam Books

industrial, monetary, social or educational strategy without long-term projections that are fed by all the necessary information on domestic or global developments and innovation[73]*"*.

This book undoubtedly deals with an unpopular subject (industrial policy). This does not mean that it is intended only for insiders or experts in deciphering "**industrial black boxes**", far from it, nor does it claim to provide answers to all industrial concerns. Yet it would be unfair to deny the existence of epistemological obstacles that readers may encounter throughout the reading. ***Some readers may use a word, an idea, a comparison, a sentence or a number to summarise the entire work.*** Besides, the propensity to distort ideas is neither neutral nor new. It draws on a limiting tendency to denigrate or manipulate, due to the difficulty of understanding, opposing an alternate project or a membership in a group whose values are defended.

Rather, this is not a call for the gullible celebration of a work that claims to be alienated from the advocacy of a widespread utopia.

The publication of this book could also trigger the unleashing of threats secreted by ideologies that convey prejudices, fanaticism, fantasies and superiority or inferiority of knowledge complexes, which have made the world vulnerable to crises and divisions and have rendered it more selfish and dangerous. Fortunately, the majority of people will approach it with a benevolent intellectual curiosity. So much the better!

The debate is therefore open and, according to Charles Maurras: *"Nothing is done without criticism, without*

[73] Pisar S. « La Ressource Humaine » (The Human Resource)

faith[74]*"*; and indicates with a note of humour: *"It takes nothing to destroy. It takes years of effort, labour and patience to create. The filthy breath of a schemer is enough to ruin*[75]*"*. Of course, being open to criticism does not mean spreading endless and fruitless polemics, hence another warning by C. Maurras: *"The art of dragging the discussion between those who know and those who do not know is the most elementary of all arts. We practised it in secondary school: But ... Then ... So ... If ... All it takes is three little words ten times and twenty times repeated. No doubt knowledge is equipped to dispel one by one these ill-willed doubts. However, this tedious work represents a huge waste of time, not to mention the undermining of trust.*[76]*"*

The author thus aimed at countering the inevitable spiral of doom and gloom in intellectual production, enticing complex or irritable ideologists and scientists, reassuring the timid and discouraging the schemers. **Then? Let there be debate!**

[74] Maurras C.; Mes Idées Politiques (1937 "My Political thoughts"); pp. 169; 175 ; 183.
[74] Idem.
[75] Idem.
[76].Ibid.

GENERAL CONCLUSION

While the debate is still in its infancy and Cameroon's industrial history remains an entirely open field of investigation, would it be possible to reach a conclusion on such a vast subject in a sole publication?

The initial aim was to revisit the country's industrial performance and assess its chances of emergence in terms of policies, discourse and action. Cameroon's economic growth path through the two (02) quadrennial plans, the six (06) five-year programmes, the structural adjustment programme and the master plan for industrialisation, could not trigger the expected industrial progress. Likewise, Vision 2035, GESP and NDS 30 are far from being a revenge on history.

A summary review of the industrial models of certain countries will have made it possible to avoid any form of dogmatism and embroilment in theories which, despite their relevance, do not provide a complete solution to all situations. Hence, the attempt to invoke a utopia in the sense of Victor Hugo: "Utopia is the truth of tomorrow" or of Lamartine: "Utopias are only premature truths". Moreover, we affirm with Jean Coussy (2005) that:

"The literature on development has long been a series of mutual trials on the responsibility for failures. Today the situation has changed on two points:

- *There are spectacular growth successes, particularly in Asia ;*

- *Successful catching up has been achieved on eclectic policies (those borrowing from the most opposing doctrines).*

It now seems less useful to pursue polemics between theories than to identify, in each theory, the part of truth, its places and times of relevance[77]*"*. From this view point, every school of thought, whether realistic, liberal or Marxist, has committed errors. Our eclectic and heterodox approach will have influenced the conceptual and theoretical neutrality of this project. The reference to numerous concepts was intended to open the way to strategic innovation and instrumental optimisation that would allow public or private economic actors to fully play their part.

Certainly, this volume's variety of sequences and percussion will be striking to the reader's attention; but how could one escape the temptation to press several keys on the keyboard when the concert of industrial policies is in full swing?

Having with no doubt the pretence of challenging an institution (Vision 2035, GESP and NDS 30) and its powerful elite (the high-ranking officials of economic administrations), this essay is poised to confront any desecration of these sacred texts. Fortunately, many of the temple guardians have revised their position in view of the poor economic performance recorded and the industrial slippage of the growth path outlined. Of course, we are not harbouring the illusion of writing a Vulgate, but rather reconstructing the trajectories that were used to steer Cameroonian industry on sight and making a prognosis about its resilience. Emergence could come **by 2035**

[77] Jean Coussy in "La Place des Pays tard venus au Développement" (Challenges for Late Developing countries). P. Berthaud and Kebabdjian.

according to the State vision, or later; but none of these prophecies is self-fulfilling.

The period leading up to this deadline is therefore that of difficult choices; "*in periods of transition, history always hesitates between the rebound made possible by horizontal social cohesion or the growth crisis whose outcome is imposed by vertical order*[78]". This is why we have suggested, like Olivier Passet, the use of one of the **industrial strike forces**, massive support for a few **national champions** capable of driving major programmes and facing up to competition.

Michaëlle Jean, Secretary General of the Francophonie, prefers to talk of "**Massive Building Forces**[79]**".** Recourse to industrial strike forces within the framework of a **State of Industrial Emergency**, can make the emergence of Cameroon possible; but only if bureaucratic centralism, incompetence and corruption, inertia and selfishness that undermine institutions and governance are dismantled. It is therefore necessary to move the lines that have succeeded in sealing even the most daring, patriotic initiatives, and add to faith, work; fight hard. Very hard! That is, without distraction, nostalgia or complex, because emergence can only be achieved if men and women of all ages agree to reinvent themselves individually and collectively, learning from the trial and error, successes and failures of the past.

Wavering steps based on economic principles tested in different contexts and times could only lead to a rupture between the industrial and social spheres. Consequently, successive governments have set the pace of an

---

78 .Bouchet, Michel-Henry in "Globalisation : Introduction à l'Economie du Nouveau Monde (An Introduction to the Economy of the New World); Paris, 2005.

79 Michaëlle Jean, in a keynote address as she was awarded Doctor Honoris Causa by the University of Yaounde I on 15-04-15.

administration that was early infected with the viruses of cumbersomeness and unconcern that have undermined efficiency and creativity. And, the time of the politician being reputed to be short (although very long in Cameroon), bureaucracy has been able to enforce its own, the long-term time.

For John Maynard Keynes, policy makers limited achievements are not surprising: *"The master-economist must possess a rare combination of gifts .... He must be mathematician, historian, statesman, philosopher—in some degree. He must study the present in the light of the past for the purposes of the future. He must be purposeful and disinterested in a simultaneous mood, as aloof and incorruptible as an artist, yet sometimes as near to earth as a politician[80] ."*

It is therefore not easy to be an accomplished economist, and above all, an industrial economist; but this fear of the subject did not prevent Keynes from becoming the theorist whose theses continue to dominate economic history with an undoubted authority.

2035 or 2050 is tomorrow for some, or too far away for others. But in the meantime, "**let's rise and shine**"! With METHODS, please! Cameroon needs **Captains, conundrums, icons of industry** to sound the death knell of an era, the era of fuzzy, corrupt and corrupted businessmen, bulimic accumulators of fortunes to secure themselves and their siblings by selling overpriced and poor quality services to managers plundering the public goods they are supposed to protect.

---

[80] J.M. Keynes, quoted by Renato Di Ruzza: Stories, Knowledge and Power in Political Economy; Economic Studies and Documents. Printed by: Imprimerie SADAG, 01200 Bellegarde, Sept. 1990.

The performance we should pursue is eloquently recalled by Samuel PISAR who, drawing lessons from history, wished that each country should have its own landmarks and symbols. Referring to a famous telephone exchange between two political leaders, one day, the United States President, Richard Nixon, called the Israeli Head of Government, Golda Meir, and said:

"Madam Prime Minister, you have a remarkable army. At home, things are going rather badly. Can you send me three of your Generals, for instance Moshe Dayan, Ezer Weitzman, and Ariel Sharon? Reply from Madame Golda Meir: *"Mr. President, I'll do everything I can to help you. I will send you my three Generals. In exchange, I ask you for three of yours:* General Motors, General Electric and General Food.[81]"

Whether this conversation is real or conceived by a fertile mind, the truth is therein, that brain capital remains the main wealth of nations. It is thus on our individual, corporative and institutional capacities that we are betting on competitiveness for the industrialisation of Cameroon. /

---

[81] Pisar S., in "The Human Resource".

BIBLIOGRAPHY

Ansoff I. (1989) ; Corporation Development Strategy, assisted by Edward I. McDonnell ; revised by Marie Waquet,The French Editions, 1989.

Archier G., Sérieyx H. (1984): ''The 3rd-Type Entreprise''; Edition du Seuil, Paris, France.

Babikoussana ; Abissama Onana, (2004) «Cameroon and Africa's Economic Debates» ; forwarded by Célestin Ndonga ; Prescriptor, Yaoundé, Cameroun.

Baker R., (2008), Illicit Financial Flows from Africa; Hidden Resources for Development; Global Financial Integrity. Site www.gfig.org.

Bartoli M. (1994): ''Entreprise Diagnostic. InterEditions, Paris, France.

Berthaud P.; Kébabdjian G. (2006): ''The Policy Issue in International Economy''. Collection « Recherches ». La Découverte Edition, Paris, France.

Bessis S. (1991): ''Hunger in the World''. Edition la Découverte, Paris V, France.

Bissek P. (1994): Habitat and Democratization in Cameroon, Karthala, France.

Bouchet M-H. (2005) : la Globalization ; Introduction to the New World Economy, Pearson Education, France.

Bourcier J-P. (1991): The New Gurus; Advisors, Consultants, Experts…They are everywhere; Ed. Ramsay, Paris-VI, France.

Boyer L.: Equilbey N., (2003); ''Organization, Theories, Application''. New Editions of Organization. France.

Bruchey S. ; The Foundations of a Free Economy Dynamism » ; book published under the title: « The Roots of American Economic Growth 1607- 1861 ; published by Harper & Row, Publishers, New York City, N.Y. ; An Essay on Social Findings. The French translation in 1985 by George de Dehn, is prefaced by Mathieu Onambélé Ekani, Journalist, specialized in African Economic Issues.

Carlton D. et Perloff J. (1998) ; Economie Industrielle ; édition De Boeck.

Cinquième Plan Quinquennal de Développement Economique, Social et Culturel (1981); United Republic of Cameroon ; Ministry of Economy and Planning ; Yaoundé National Printing, Cameroon.

Coutrot T.; Husson M. (1993): « The Destinies of the Third World ». Analysis, Results and Outlook. Editions Nathan, Paris, France.

De Bernis G.; (1988): « Economic Theories and the Functioning of the World Economy »; Grenoble University Press; France.

The Second Five-Year Plan on Economic and Social Development (July 1966); Federal Republic of Cameroon; SOPECAM.

Di Ruzza R. (1988): Elements of Epistemology for Economists. Grenoble University Press, France.

Chesnais F. (1997): « The Globalization the Capital»; updated new Edition; Alternatives Economiques, Syros, Paris, France.

D'Iribarne A. (1989); Competitiveness. Social Challenge, Educational Stake. CNRS Press, France.

Drullion K.; (2005): « NGOs, New Sentinels for the Reputation of Enterprises ». Professional Master's Degree Thesis; School of Higher Studies on Information and Communication. Paris IV Université La Sorbonne CELSA, France.

Frantz J. (2010); Governance and Social Corporation's Responsibility; Levers of Growth for the Intermediary Sized enterprises. Report adopted in October the 7th 2010 during the General Assembly of the Paris Chamber of Trade and Industry; Paris, France.

Gauthier B. (1996); "Dynamics of the Manufacturing African Sector in Structural Adjustment Period: The Case of Cameroon "; publication in the Regional Development n°3 Review; Montréal, Canada.

Genthon C., (1995): Growth and Crisis in the World Computer Industry; Paris, Syros, France.

Gereffi, G. (1994): The Organization of Buyer-Driven Global Commodity Chains: ''How U.S. Retailers Shape Overseas Production Networks'', in Gereffi G. and M. Korzeniewicz

Gninkam E. et Totale E., (2009), a Report written for HELIO International on Energy Systems: Vulnerability-Adaptation- Resilience (VAR); Sub-Saharan Africa, Cameroon.

Gilder G. (1981): Wealth & Poverty. Translated from American by Pierre-Emmanuel Dauzat. Albin Michel, Paris.

Hugon P., (2011) « After the Crisis, a new Development Paradigm? »; article published in Problèmes économiques N° 3 011, of January 19, 2011. Paris, La Documentation Française.

Institut National de la Statistique (2011), General Census of Enterprises (GCE 2009) ; Thematic Report, novembre 2011.

Jeune Afrique (2013) ; Hors-Série n°32, Paris, France.

Keynes J.M., (1936); the General Theory of Employment, Interest and Money. Translated in 1985 from English by Largentaye ; Payot, Paris, France.

La Documentation Française n° 243, October- December 1989: « Strategies Industrielles Mondiales »; « Cahiers Français » on the direction of Marguerite Boucher. France, 1990.

Marion A. : Le Diagnostic d'Entreprise. Collection Gestion ; Ed. Economica, Paris, 1993.

Stratégie Nationale de Lutte Contre la Corruption du Cameroun 2010-2015.

Markell, P. and Malmberg, A. (1999): Localized Learning and Industrial Competitiveness. Cambridge Journal of Economics, 1999? 23? 167-185

Maurras C. (1993); « My Political Ideas ». Preface of Pierre Gaxotte of the French Academy. Text established by Pierre Chardon ; Albatros Editions.

Morvan Y. ; Fondements de l'Economie Industrielle, 2ème édition. Ed. Economica, 1991.

Nana-Sinkam S.C. (1999): « Cameroon in the Globalization; Conditions and Premises for a Sustainable Development ». Edition CLE, Yaoundé,Cameroon..

Organization for Economic and Cooperation for Development (2003): Electronic Trade and Development; under the direction of Andrea Goldstein O'Connor. OECD.

Oyono D. (1992): Colony or International Mandate? The French Policy in Cameroon from 1919 to1946. Editions LHarmattan, Paris, France.

Penda Ekoka C. (1997); Cameroon: Toward the Third Millennium; Preface by Joseph Charles Doumba ; Editions EDI'ACTION ; Yaoundé, Cameroun.

Perrin J., (1984) : The Technological Transfers ; La Découverte Editions, Paris. Second édition.

Pettang C. (1999): Habitat & Urban Development, volume II; Elements to Optimize the Production of Decent Habitat in Cameroon; Yaoundé University Press, Cameroun.

Pisar S. (1983): »The Human Resource ». Jean-Claude Lattès Editions, France.

Porter M. (1987): « Stategic Choices and Competition ». Techniques of Sector and Competition Analysis in Industry. Translated by Philippe Lavergne ; revision of Georges Sudrie ; Economica, Paris, 1990; Dunod, France.

Porter M.; (1986): « The Competitive Advantage ». How to forestall their Competitors and hold down the lead? Translated from American by Philippe de Lavergne; InterEditions, Paris, France.

The first 5-Years Economic and Social Development Plan (July 1961); The Republic of Cameroon; The Ministry of Economy and Planning. Yaoundé.

Ramsey, S., Esquisse de L'Economie Américaine ; U.S. Information Agency, 1991.

République du Cameroun : Document de Stratégie pour la Croissance et l'Emploi ; cades de référence de l'action gouvernementale pour la période 2010-2020 ; Août 2009.

Samuelson A., (1991): Contemporary International Economy; Real and Monetary Aspects; Grenoble University Press.

Savas, E.S. (2002): Privatizations and Public-Private Partnerships. Translation from American by Michel Le Seac'h; Nouveaux Horizons, ARS, Paris, France.

Scarborough, Norman S.; Cornwall Jeffrey (2016); Essentials of Entrepreneurship and Small Business. Eight Edition, Pearson.

Severino J-M; Jacquet P. (2002); Development Aid, A Public Policy in the core of Sustainable Development and of the Governance of the Globalization. The Financial and Economic Review n°66.

Sixth 5-Years Economic, Social and Cultural Development Plan (July 1986); Republic of Cameroon; Ministry of Planning and Regional Development; National Printing Press; Yaoundé.

Tamokwé Paptié G. B.; (2003): Globalization and Diversification in the Cameroon Industrial Apparatus. Ph.D Thesis in Economics; University of de Douala, Year 2003/2004. Cameroun

Tandon Yash ; (2008): Ending Aid Dependence ; foreword by former President of Tanzania; Fahamus Books. Printed in United Kingdom; South Centre Publications; 2008.

The World Bank (July 2012); Cameroon Economic Update: Stepping out into the World; with focus on the Trade Facilitation. Issue N° 4; Country Office, Yaoundé, Cameroon.

The World Bank (2018); Cameroon Public Expenditure Review. Aligning Expenditure with the Goals of Vision 2035. Country Office, Yaoundé, Cameroon.

Third 5-Years Economic and Social Development Plan (July 1971); Republic of Cameroon; Ministry of Planning and Regional Development; SOPECAM Editions, Yaoundé, Cameroon.

Todorov B., ISO 9000, une force de management ; Gaëtan Morin éditeur, 1997.

Toffler A.; (1991): **THE NEW POWERS**. Knowledge, Wealth, and Violence at the Eve of the XXI Century;

translated from US English by André Charpentier, with the collaboration of Denise Meunier, Evelyne Chatelain, Chicheportiche, Eric Diacon ; Fayard Editions, Paris, France.

Tomasz Siudek, Aldona Zawojska (2014): Competitiveness in the Economic Concepts. Theories and Empirical Research. Warsaw University of Life Science-SGGW. Oeconomica 13 (1) 2014, 91- 108. Scientarum Polonium. Poland.

United Nations Industrial Development Organization (UNIDO): Industrial Performance and Capabilities of Cameroon; analysis of industrial sector.

Valère E. ; (1989): Le Chantier de l'Avenir. Entretiens avec Samuel Pisar. Collection les Grands Entretiens, dirigée par Jean-Louis Gouraud. Editions Favre, 1989.

Wriggins H. /Gunnar A-K, (1980): The North-South Dialogue and the Poverty Reduction. Translation of de Jean Daché ; Economica, Paris, France.

http://students.aiu.edu/submissions/profiles/resources/onlineBook/W8z3L4_Essentials_of_Entrepreneurship_and_Small_Business_Management-_8.pdf
http://ec.europa.eu/europe2020/making-it-happen/
https://www.ecb.europa.eu/pub/economic-research/research networks/html/researcher_compnet.en.html;

TABLE OF CONTENTS

Structures éditoriales du groupe L'Harmattan

L'Harmattan Italie
Via degli Artisti, 15
10124 Torino
harmattan.italia@gmail.com

L'Harmattan Hongrie
Kossuth l. u. 14-16.
1053 Budapest
harmattan@harmattan.hu

L'Harmattan Sénégal
10 VDN en face Mermoz
BP 45034 Dakar-Fann
senharmattan@gmail.com

L'Harmattan Cameroun
TSINGA/FECAFOOT
BP 11486 Yaoundé
inkoukam@gmail.com

L'Harmattan Burkina Faso
Achille Somé – tengnule@hotmail.fr

L'Harmattan Guinée
Almamya, rue KA 028 OKB Agency
BP 3470 Conakry
harmattanguinee@yahoo.fr

L'Harmattan RDC
185, avenue Nyangwe
Commune de Lingwala – Kinshasa
matangilamusadila@yahoo.fr

L'Harmattan Congo
67, boulevard Denis-Sassou-N'Guesso
BP 2874 Brazzaville
harmattan.congo@yahoo.fr

L'Harmattan Mali
ACI 2000 - Immeuble Mgr Jean Marie Cisse
Bureau 10
BP 145 Bamako-Mali
mali@harmattan.fr

L'Harmattan Togo
Djidjole – Lomé
Maison Amela
face EPP BATOME
ddamela@aol.com

L'Harmattan Côte d'Ivoire
Résidence Karl – Cité des Arts
Abidjan-Cocody
03 BP 1588 Abidjan
espace_harmattan.ci@hotmail.fr

Nos librairies en France

Librairie internationale
16, rue des Écoles
75005 Paris
librairie.internationale@harmattan.fr
01 40 46 79 11
www.librairieharmattan.com

Librairie des savoirs
21, rue des Écoles
75005 Paris
librairie.sh@harmattan.fr
01 46 34 13 71
www.librairieharmattansh.com

Librairie Le Lucernaire
53, rue Notre-Dame-des-Champs
75006 Paris
librairie@lucernaire.fr
01 42 22 67 13

www.ingramcontent.com/pod-product-compliance
Lightning Source LLC
Chambersburg PA
CBHW071443230926
51846CB00001B/329